TEACHERS HELPING TEACHERS SERIES

A Portfolio of Teaching Ideas

For High School Biology

TEACHERS HELPING TEACHERS SERIES

A Portfolio of Teaching Ideas

For High School Biology

Editor: Professor Don Galbraith
Writers: Honour Specialist Biology Candidates
Faculty of Education, University of Toronto

TRIFOLIUM BOOKS INC.

Trifolium Books Inc.
A Fitzhenry & Whiteside Company
195 Allstate Parkway
Markham, Ontario, Canada L3R 4T8

Safety: The activities in this book are safe when carried out in an organized, structured setting. Please ensure you provide to your students specific information about the safety routines used in your school. It is, of course, critical to assess your students' level of responsibility in determining which activities to use. As well, please make sure that your students know where all the safety equipment is, and how to use it. If you are not completely familiar with the safety requirements for the use of specialized equipment and your school's policy on disposal of chemicals, please ensure that you consult with school authorities before students conduct the experiments. The publisher and authors can accept no responsibility for any damage caused or sustained by use or misuse of ideas or materials mentioned in this book.

Care has been taken to trace ownership of copyright material contained in this book. The publishers will gladly receive any information that will enable them to rectify any reference or credit line in subsequent editions.

Canadian Cataloguing in Publication Data
A portfolio of teaching ideas for high school biology

(Teachers helping teachers)
ISBN 1-895579-91-0

1. Biology - Study and teaching (Secondary).
I. Galbraith, Donald I., 1936-

QH315.P67 1996   574'.071'2   C96-930696-2

Printed and bound in Canada
10 9 8 7 6 5 4

This book's text stock contains more than 50% recycled paper.

Editor: Rosemary Tanner
Project coordinator,
 designer: Diane Klim
Cover designer, Fizzz Design Inc.
 production coordinator: Francine Geraci

Table of Contents

Introduction
&
Acknowledgments

Where do people get the idea to write a book or start a project or found a new organization? How do things begin? This endeavor was begun at the Honor Specialist Biology course, held at the University of Toronto's Faculty of Education in July, 1995. (This is a course for teachers who wish to upgrade their biology-teaching skills.) One course requirement was to produce an "original" biology problem. These problems, of course, were exchanged with classmates. But why stop there? Since we are all struggling to improve our teaching, to make our lessons more interesting and challenging, why not share the ideas beyond the confines of a summer course? Out of this came the idea to gather, edit, and publish the collective efforts of the teachers attending this course. Given that no individual contributed more than a few pages to the project, we agreed to turn over any royalties to the Hospital for Sick Children in Toronto. Trudy Rising of Trifolium Books Inc., a leader in publishing innovative materials for the classroom, consented (in a moment of weakness) to publish the material in an easy, classroom-ready format.

In today's busy world, we no longer have the luxury of being able to "go it alone." Our strength is our collective strength, helping and supporting one another to make every classroom a better classroom. Perhaps this will be the first of many similar projects. Many thanks to all who participated — the teacher authors (whose names appear next to their activities in the Table of Contents), and the staff at Trifolium. If you have any comments, activities, or ideas that you would like to share, send them to me, Don Galbraith, c/o Ontario Institute for Studies in Education/University of Toronto (OISE/UT), 371 Bloor Street West, Toronto, Ontario, Canada, M5S 2R7. Who knows, maybe there will be a *Portfolio of Teaching Ideas for High School Biology II*.

To the Teacher

Biology can be and should be an exciting, vibrant subject to study. What could be more interesting than life itself! Regrettably, more often than we care to acknowledge, the study of biology is presented as a rhetoric of conclusions, as a compilation of definitions, and formulas, and facts. This modest book is an attempt to provide variety to the teaching of topics common to every biology curriculum. Designed for any course of study, the activities have been classified according to general biological topics.

This book is not intended to replace the resources that you might be using presently. Instead, it can supplement and complement your program. As you examine each activity, consider how it might be used to enhance those presently being used. As we all know, in an education setting as in life itself, variety is, indeed, a key to success.

A Problem-Solving Approach

A cursory examination of the contents will reveal that the activities differ from many found in traditional lab activity books. Firstly, the activities attempt to present common topics of study in creative ways, engaging students by using everyday situations and scenarios. The activities often require the students to apply some of the knowledge they possess to solve a problem or to discover who committed a crime. (Most of us are criminologists at heart!) Secondly, the activities are student-driven. Rather than giving the students information, the activities require them to figure things out for themselves. Thirdly, and perhaps most importantly, students are given practice solving both quantitative and qualitative problems. Certainly, most teachers (and students) of biology would agree that there is a real need for more quantitative problems in the study of this science. This book, then, attempts to address this deficiency. Having said this, it should be clear that not all problem-solving involves the use of numbers and tables of data.

After your students have tackled some of these activities, we hope that they will be motivated to look at different ways of approaching the material that they study in class. And there is still so much that needs to be done beyond the classroom. May your students, as members of the next generation, acquire the skills and knowledge to work on some of the world's exciting questions and pressing problems. Good luck!

The Authors

Features of This Book

As you use this book, please note the following organizational features. Under each general topic, you will find different types of activities and exercises.

Student Activity

These activities usually have two parts: a **Teacher Background** and one or more student pages. The **Teacher Background** often includes materials, notes on techniques, anticipated student answers to the associated activity, and assessment strategies. This material is not included for all activities, just where the authors considered it necessary.

The accompanying Student Activity may be photocopied only by the teacher who purchases the book, and only for the use of his or her students. The book has been three-hole punched for ease in dividing it into sections for use, along with other materials, in a resource binder.

Teacher Activity

A few of the activities are best described as teacher-directed. It is intended that the teacher organize and direct the activity in a more traditional manner. However, even these activities lend themselves to a problem-solving exercise for the students.

Occasionally, you will find an activity which has no teacher resource material associated with it. Don't overlook these; they offer good ideas to use with your students. And you will find, as well, a number of activities that are simply good ideas, ways for students to organize their own learning (e.g., "Graphic Organizers") or ways for teachers to introduce topics.

Problem Solving in Biology

The activities in this book give your students an opportunity to do some problem-solving in biology. When most students think of problem-solving, particularly as it relates to school work, they think of numbers and formulas. But problems come in all shapes and sizes. Some do involve numbers and graphs and calculations. Many others require them to write explanations, to use logic, and to share ideas with other students. These activities are intended to give your students practice working their way through different types of problems, problems that relate to topics which they are studying in biology.

With any problem-solving activity, it important to approach the solution in an orderly fashion. Not all problems can be solved in the same way. However, the questions on the following page might help in your students' search for answers. You might wish to use the page as a handout for student use and as a guide for class discussions.

Activity Guide

1. What am I trying to find out?

2. What information is given that can will help me solve the problem? Note that some problems include information you do *not* need.

3. What background knowledge do I have that I can I apply to solve the problem? Problem-solving does require background knowledge (and, often, some specific skills). If you have a clear understanding of the topic, in general, you'll be in a better position to solve the problem.

4. Where can I turn to get more information about the topic? There are many sources of information, including any or all of the following:

   a) *Textbooks:* Don't overlook the obvious — go to standard textbooks. Do make use of indices and glossaries!

   b) *Libraries:* Libraries of today, including your school library, contain much more than books and journals. If your school library has a CD-ROM player and computer which can be used to search for information about a topic, it will significantly reduce the amount of time required to find information. Don't let the technology intimidate you. If you have not yet used a CD for this purpose, you will be pleasantly surprised how easy it is to master.

   c) *Journals:* There are many fine science magazines and journals and your school or community library will probably have a few. Many journals have an annual index of all topics covered each year in the final issue for that year. For example, the December issue of *Scientific American* has a complete list of articles and topics for that year.

   d) *Newspapers:* Newspapers offer an often overlooked source of information. Sometimes, however, the articles are written for the general public, and might lack the detail which you might require for a topic.

   e) *The Internet:* This is, of course, the new "window on the world," via a vast network of computers which can communicate electronically with one another. If you or your school have access to the Internet, do make use of it. "Netscape," a very popular software package for both Mac and IBM computers, makes it possible to search for information on a topic right around the globe. Check Appendix D, entitled "Biology and the Internet," for a number of World Wide Web sites dedicated to science research and information at all levels of complexity.

5. Depending upon the topic, what information can I gain from or share with my peers?

6. How can I best present the solution to my problem? If appropriate, make use of visuals, charts, graphs, etc. to represent the solution to your problem.

Section 1
Cells and Cell Chemistry

Student Activity 1.1 pH and Enzyme Function

Teacher Background

Introduction

This assignment consists of exposing an enzyme (catalase) of baker's yeast *(Saccharomyces cerevisiae)* to a variety of pH solutions to see which pH environment provides the ideal condition for the enzyme to carry out its function. Quantitative as well as qualitative data can be obtained from the experiment.

Purpose

The experiment has many purposes; the most obvious is to have students see that catalase functions best (with respect to the production of CO_2) at a particular pH level. The more subtle purposes are as follows: (a) to offer an experimental introduction to the connection between enzyme structure (primary, secondary, tertiary, quaternary) and function, (b) to have the students actually see evidence of a microorganism at work, (c) to gather, evaluate, and present both quantitative and qualitative data, and (d) to have the students experience an open-ended experiment with numerous possible extensions and levels of understanding.

Additional Suggestions

1. The introduction and use of pH meters can be taught before the students do the experiment.
2. A common and often large source of error in this experiment is the use of irregularly shaped disks of filter paper. To avoid this problem, make certain the students carefully examine the disks they use to ensure they are properly and consistently sized.
3. Drug-store 3% hydrogen peroxide is fine for this experiment. Prepare a 1:1000 dilution of it using ordinary tap water. Depending on the freshness of the H_2O_2 solution, you may have to dilute it further. I suggest testing it prior to the experiment. It should take about 40 to 60 s for the disk to rise to the surface from the time it first contacts the bottom of the beaker.
4. To prepare the pH solutions (pH 3, 5, 7, 9, 11) required for the experiment, use 1.0 m HCl and 1.0 m NaOH to adjust the pH of the dilute hydrogen peroxide solutions. Because this takes some time and also because of the potential danger of the acid and base solutions, do not let the students do this. (Note: other strengths of HCl and NaOH may be used instead.)
5. When the students fill the beakers with the different pH solutions, ensure that each is filled to the same level. This practice removes any source of experimental error caused by different levels.
6. Mix the yeast with 1 L of lukewarm water.

Possible Extensions

1. Have the students graph their results using Lotus 123 or some other database software package.
2. Have the students research the four levels of structure of an enzyme and relate the importance of structure to function.
3. As a group or individually, have the students research a topic such as "alcohol consumption and urination" (i.e., try to have the students make the connection between alcohol and enzyme denaturation, and examine the effect alcohol has on the body.)
4. If you have a particularly keen group of individuals who wish to investigate the experiment further, have them repeat the lab, altering the temperature or enzyme concentration (other possibilities exist).

Student Activity 1.1 pH and Enzyme Function

Purpose

The purpose of this experiment is to investigate the connection between the pH environment and an enzyme's ability to function properly.

Apparatus

hydrogen peroxide (3%)
hydrochloric acid
sodium hydroxide
1 L flask
pH meter
safety goggles
gloves and aprons (optional)
1 envelope of common baker's
   yeast diluted in 1 L lukewarm H_2O
filter paper (number three)
hole punch
tweezers
500 mL beaker
5 beakers of matching size and shape
stopwatch

Method

1. Using the hole punch and the filter paper, punch out 15 disks of filter paper. Make certain they are all of uniform size.
2. Label the 5 beakers "pH 3," "pH 5," "pH 7," "pH 9," and "pH 11." Pour the appropriate pH solution into each beaker to the same depth.
3. Place a small sample of the prepared baker's yeast solution in a beaker and place the 15 disks in it. Allow the disks to soak in the solution for a few minutes.
4. Using tweezers, take one of the disks out of the yeast solution, and put it at the bottom of the prepared beaker labelled pH 3. When the disk makes contact with the bottom of the beaker, start your stopwatch. You will observe small bubbles forming on the disk, and the disk will eventually start to rise towards the surface. Stop the stopwatch when the disk just reaches the surface of the liquid. Record the time.
5. Remove the disk and rinse and dry the tweezers.
6. Repeat steps 4 & 5 a total of three times for each of the five beakers.
7. After you have all the required data, clean up your work station thoroughly and put away all equipment that you used.

Questions

1. Using proper graph paper (not quad paper), produce a graph of time vs pH. Plot the average time of the three trials for each pH solution.
2. Based on the graph, what is the optimum pH for the enzyme? At what pH did the disks take the longest time to rise to the surface?
3. Why is it advisable to have the same depth of liquid in each of the five beakers?
4. What would be the effect of altering the temperature of the experimental solutions? Design a simple experiment to discover that effect.
5. State two other common situations in which pH has an effect on an enzyme.

Teacher Activity 1.2 Mitotic Cell Division

This Cooperative Learning activity would fit well into an introductory cell unit in a biology course, or it could be used as a review activity. This should not be the first time students encounter the material.

Assessment should be twofold. Collect and mark the final diagrams, based on a rating scale made from the information given in the print material handed out. To assess group work skills, target one skill, such as "no put downs." At the end of this activity, have the students complete both a self-evaluation activity and, in the expert groups, a peer evaluation activity (perhaps a pie chart with respect to contribution to the process, and a rubric specific to the group work skill). Both of these evaluations could be placed in the students' portfolios.

Instructions

Explain that this is a jigsaw/gallery walk activity that will review and assess their learning of the different stages of cell division. Working together with other students they will be expected to be able to describe clearly to others one stage in the process of mitosis.

1. Form Home groups of 5. Number off. Provide Reading Material *Cell Division* and explain that this outlines what you will look for when you evaluate the diagrams. Set a time for the Expert group work that is appropriate for your class.

2. Form Expert groups. *(Make efforts toward heterogeneity here. You could base the group selection on their marks, with some effort to make groups that will function well.)* Assign each Expert group one stage of mitosis. In Expert groups, the students discuss the material and produce a labelled diagram of the assigned stage of mitosis. *[The students could use cooperative learning group roles here, such as materials person (together the group could even determine materials to use to produce an excellent representation of the stage for which they are responsible); encourager; time keeper; drawer(s) and labellers; and presenter]*

3. Return print materials.

4. Reform Home groups. Travel to each diagram and have the member of the appropriate Expert group explain the stage to the Home group. Home group members should question and give feedback.

5. Return to Expert group to make any adjustments to the diagram. Complete self and group peer evaluations.

6. Hand in all products for assessment.

Teaching Notes

_____

_____

_____

_____

_____

_____

_____

_____

_____

_____

Reading Material — **Mitotic Cell Division**

Interphase

Cells are in this stage most of the time. It is often called the "resting stage" because it does not look like much is happening. However, during interphase, cells are growing and performing other activities. Most important to us today is the fact that the cell is preparing for mitosis. The cell does this by duplicating (making a second copy of) its chromatin.

Produce complete diagrams of both a plant and an animal cell in interphase. Include and label the cell membrane, nuclear membrane, nucleolus, and chromatin strands in the nucleoplasm, centrioles, and the cell wall (where appropriate).

Prophase

During prophase, the chromatin strands coil up like springs to form pairs of sister chromatids (they are called sisters because they are identical). Each pair of chromatids are joined together by a small structure called the centromere. The nuclear membrane and the nucleolus break down and disappear. In animal cells, the two centrioles split and move toward opposite poles of the cell. The centrioles appear to be joined by spindle fibers.

Produce complete diagrams of both a plant and an animal cell in prophase. Include labels for cell wall, cell membrane, chromatids, centromere, cytoplasm, centrioles, and spindle fibers (where appropriate).

Metaphase

During metaphase, the centrioles are at the poles of the animal cell. The spindle fibers extend from one centriole to the other. The sister chromatid pairs line up at the equator of the cell and the centromeres attach to spindle fibers.

Produce complete diagrams of both a plant and an animal cell in metaphase. Include labels for cell wall, cell membrane, chromatids, centromere, centrioles, and spindle fibers (where appropriate).

Anaphase

During anaphase, the centromeres split apart and the sister chromatids separate from each other and move toward opposite poles. The spindle fibers contract, moving the chromatids toward the poles.

Produce complete diagrams of both a plant and an animal cell in anaphase. Label cell wall, cell membrane, cytoplasm, centromeres, centrioles, spindle fibers, and chromatids, (where appropriate).

Telophase

Once the chromatids get to their poles, telophase begins. The chromatids unwind into chromatin strands. The nuclear membrane and nucleolus reforms. The cytoplasm divides (cytokinesis). In plant cells, a cell plate forms separating the two nuclei. In animal cells, a cleavage furrow forms around the middle of the parent cell, pinching it into two daughter cells, and the centrioles double.

Produce complete diagrams of both a plant cell and an animal cell in telophase. Label cell wall, cell membrane, cytoplasm, chromatin strands, nuclear membrane, nucleolus, cell plate, cleavage furrow, and centrioles (where appropriate).

Student Activity 1.3 Examining Bacterial Cultures

Teacher Background

Introduction

This lab provides an opportunity for students to examine their own school environment and the associated bacterial cultures that may be found there. You may want to demonstrate aseptic technique before the students start the lab. Suggest that students use a few "control" plates; one poured with agar but not reopened, and one opened for a few minutes in a busy lab. Prepare an incubator at 30°C.

The quadrants referred to below are those associated with Bernice McCarthy's identification of four student learning styles, commonly referred to as the 4MAT method. Picture a circle divided into four quarters or quadrants into which students who learn in different ways are placed. Each of the four learning styles are characterized by a question which the students in the different quadrants might ask. From quadrants one to four respectively, they are "Why?", "What?", "How?", and "If?" Take time to find out more about this approach. It makes a lot of sense.

QUADRANT 1

These types of learners often ask the question, "Why is this material important to me?" Discussion and sharing of the findings, and the organizing of the class data contribute to discovery through their personal results and connection to the larger class data set helps them to see the relevance of the content. The information obtained concretely may be manipulated and reflected upon by the quadrant 1 learner during the lab write up.

QUADRANT 2

These types of learners are concerned with what they have to learn. They tend to be quite successful in a traditional classroom. Practical activities may not seem to interest them. However, working in groups and possibly functioning as an organizer of, and collation of data should provide this student with trends and results. The opportunities for personal research through the text and interaction with the instructor should also encourage a positive learning environment for quadrant 2 learners.

QUADRANT 3

These learners find practical hands-on activities and an active exploration of their environment to be vehicles through which they can learn most comfortably. The "reality" of the presence of bacteria in their environment is often quite a discovery. This lab may lead into further exploration of bacteria using student controlled conditions, e.g. varying pH, temperature, or nutrient levels in agar. The presence or absence of antibiotics may also be explored.

QUADRANT 4

These students, most interested in self discovery, are prone to asking the question, "If I changed this, what would happen?" The answers are "different" depending on the types of cultures they grow. The relevance of the lab to their everyday environment provide opportunities to perceive concretely and process it actively through sharing and common class data.

Objectives

The objectives addressed, using this activity, are as follows:
I.   Attitudes
    A. curiosity about the diversity, structure and reproductive processes of bacteria
    B. commitment to personal hygiene, health, and food-handling habits, designed to minimize exposure to the harmful effects of some bacteria
II. Skills
    A. drawing and labelling bacteria (colonies)
    B. using proper aseptic techniques when handling bacterial cultures
    C. preparing sterilized bacterial growth media
    D. observing and describing the characteristics of bacterial growth and colony shape
III. Knowledge
    A. explain the reasons for aseptic techniques
    B. describe the use of antibiotics (if used in the lab)

Marking Scheme

It is possible to grow bacteria in the laboratory, just as though you were growing plants. Growing bacteria is called "bacterial culture." Most bacteria do not have chlorophyll and cannot make their own food. You must supply the food in the form of a nutrient-enriched "agar" jelly that has been heated (sterilized).

Bacteria placed on the agar will begin to reproduce on the rich food supply. Depending on the type of bacterium, within 15-30 minutes each cell will split into two cells. This process continues, producing many millions of cells. Usually within a day or two, the mass of growing cells becomes large enough to see with the naked eye. This mass is called a colony. Each colony consists of millions of cells, all the same type of bacterium.

Safety Note

Aseptic techniques must be followed throughout this procedure.

Materials

safety goggles and apron
disinfectant desk cleaner
sterile Petri dishes
sterile agar in a flaskgrease pencil or marker
sterile swabs
biohazard disposal bags
incubator

Method

PART 1

1. Heat agar in a boiling water bath to melt it. Wash off your desk with disinfectant desk cleaner. Wipe it dry thoroughly.

2. Take a clean Petri dish. Using a grease pencil, draw two lines on the bottom of the dish. Make sure that you write the letters in the quadrants backwards, so they are legible from the top. Turn the dish upright.

3. Obtain a flask of melted agar. Gently tilt the top of a Petri dish as seen in diagram A, and pour in enough hot agar to just cover the bottom of the plate. Quickly slide the top back into position (as in diagram B.) Let the agar solidify for 10 min. Tape the top of the Petri dish to the bottom. Your sterile culture plate is now ready for the second part of the lab.

PART 2

1. Go to various locations in the school as discussed with your teacher. Record conditions at each location.

2. Using a sterile swab, collect possible bacteria by swabbing each area. Do not touch the swab with your fingers. Place the swab back in its sterile container and label it.

3. Return to the lab, and gently swab one of the quadrants on the Petri dish with each sample (see diagram C). Replace the lid of the Petri dish. Be careful not to damage the agar jelly.

4. Discard the swabs in special disposal bags provided by your teacher.

5. Once you have collected your samples, tape the culture plate closed, turn it upside down, and return it to your teacher.

6. After a few days, examine the plates under a dissecting microscope.

Student Activity 1.3 **Examining Bacterial Cultures** (continued)

Questions

1. Your culture plates were incubated at 30°C. Why were they not incubated at 37°C? (Hint: 37°C is body temperature.)

2. Make a chart with the following headings, and record your findings for each source of contamination. A key with diagrams is shown in Figure D. Use it as a guide.

3. a. List the areas investigated by the class that showed bacterial contamination.
   b. Which of those areas showed the greatest contamination?
   c. Which showed the least?
   d. Might some areas be contaminated and not others?

4. Under favorable conditions, bacteria may reproduce as rapidly as once every twenty minutes. At this rate, how many bacteria could be produced from a single bacterium in five hours? Construct a graph of number of bacteria vs. time to represent the situation.

5. List three factors that might restrict the growth of bacteria.

6. Write a short paragraph or construct a detailed concept map, summarizing what you have learned in this investigation.

Source of Contamination	Colony	Edge	Elevation	Surface	Color

Bacterial Cultures

Some of the terminology below is normally used by a microbiologist to describe the bacterial colonies on culture plates. You might use these to describe some of the colonies you obtain on your culture plates.

1. SHAPES

punctiform

irregular

circular

filamentous

rhizoid

2. COLOR - white, pink, etc.

3. SURFACE - smooth (glistening), dry (powdery), or rough.

Student Activity 1.4   Concept Map: Biologically Important Molecules

Teacher Background

Introduction

Concept maps are useful tools that encourage students to develop relationships between the terms they study in a unit. Concept maps are examples of graphic organizers, which are designed to enable students to represent their thoughts visually.

Many excellent resources are available describing these and other useful graphic organizers.

Assessment and Evaluation

The following is one scheme that might be used to assess this and other concept maps.

CONCEPT MAP RATING SCALE

Organization	Rating			
Logical main concept	0	1	2	
General to specific	0	1	2	3
Levels of hierarchy shown	0	1	2	3
Branching demonstrated	0	1	2	3
No repetition of descriptors	0	1		
Prepositions, verbs, or adverbs for all linkages	0	1	2	3
No linking lines crossed	0	1		
Some cross linking shown	0	1	2	

Concept	Rating			
Logical relationships between descriptors	0	1	2	3
Appropriate linkage words	0	1	2	3
Logical cross linkages	0	1	2	3
Isolated specific descriptors and linkage words form a sentence	0	1	2	3

Total

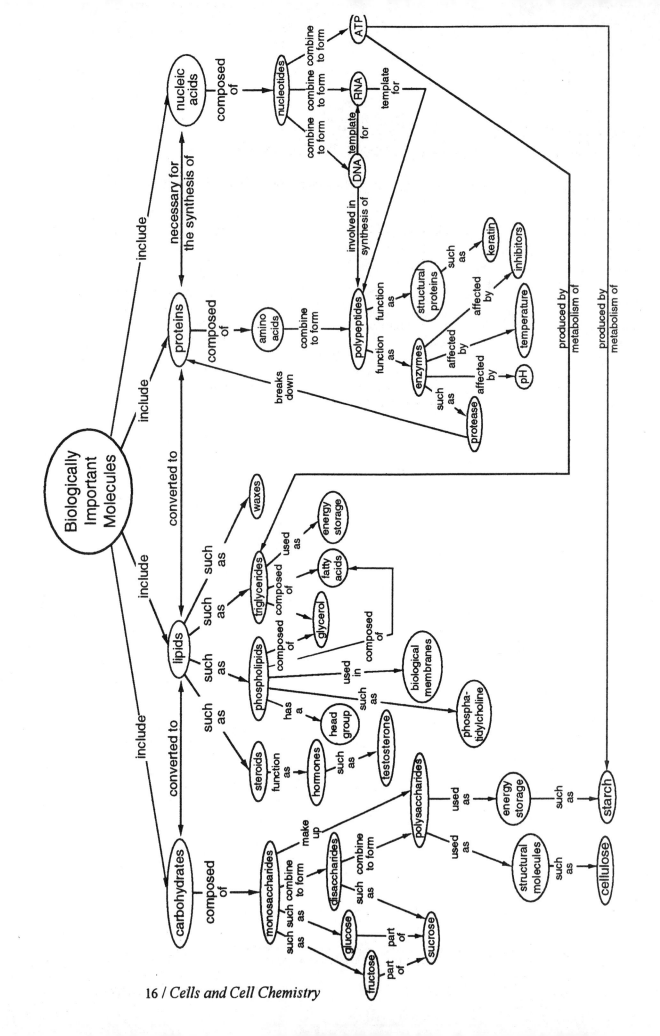

Student Activity 1.4 **Concept Map:**
Biologically Important Molecules (continued)

Develop a concept map to include the following terms that apply to the chemical basis of life.

amino acids
ATP
biological membranes
carbohydrates
cellulose
disaccharides
DNA
energy storage
enzymes
fatty acids
fructose
glucose
glycerol

head group
hormones
inhibitors
keratin
lipids
·monosaccharides
nucleic acids
nucleotides
pH
phosphatidylcholine
phospholipids
polypeptides
polysaccharides

protease
proteins
RNA
starch
steroids
structural molecules
structural proteins
sucrose
temperature
testosterone
triglycerides
waxes

Student Activity 1.5 Nutrition Concept Map

Teacher Background

Introduction

This concept map lesson is designed to help biology students organize the topic of nutrition which has a large vocabulary. The students could do this activity after they have completed the topic so that the resulting concept map can act as a visual organizer and review.

The activity is arranged as a jigsaw with each Home group having four students. The size of the Expert groups will be determined by the size of the class. If the class is very large, each Expert group could be divided into two, with both of the sub-Expert groups performing the identical task. After they finish, the subgroups may consult with each other before going to the Home group. The method for evaluation could be included with the instructions given to the students.

Assessment and Evaluation

The following is one possible method of evaluation:

Expert Group:

Map progresses from general to specific	0	1	2	3		
8-10 valid descriptors were identified	0	1	2	3	4	5
Appropriate connectors were used	0	1	2	3	4	5
Cross-linkages were logical	0	1	2			
Total:		/15				

Home Group:

Map is a single, consistent entity	1	2	3	
Additional descriptors and connectors are valid	1	2	3	
Valid modifications made to the expert group maps	1	2	3	
Map is neatly and attractively presented	1	2	3	4
Map is unique	1	2		
Total:		/15		

Anticipated Descriptors and Logical Connectors (not to be given to students)

A protein	amino acid	C lipids	fatty acids
12 non-essential	8 essential	saturated	unsaturated
complete	e.g., dairy products/ eggs/meat	glycerol	phospholipids
		sterols	e.g., cholesterol
incomplete	e.g., beans/yams/nuts	energy	cell membrane
made by organisms	must be eaten	water	special nutrient
energy	muscle		
B carbohydrates	simple	D micronutrient	no energy
complex	monosaccharides	vitamins	water-soluble
disaccharides	starch	e.g., vitamin C	lipid-soluble
glycogen	cellulose	e.g., vitamin A/E/D	minerals
plants	animals	organic	inorganic
storage	energy	cofactors	deficiency diseases

Student Activity 1.5 Nutrition Concept Map

Objective

To construct a concept map on the topic of nutrition.

Procedure

1. Form Home groups with four students in the group. Each member of the group should choose one of the following topics in which to become an expert. (2 min)
   A: proteins
   B: carbohydrates
   C: lipids and water (2 concept maps)
   D: micronutrients

2. Meet the other members of your Expert group at the location indicated by the appropriate letter, i.e., A, B, C, or D. In your Expert group, construct a concept map for your topic using at least 10 descriptors with logical connectors. Hand in one copy of the Expert group concept map, and each person take a copy of the map to the Home group. (20 min)

3. Reform your Home groups and construct a large concept map that includes the information from the concept maps constructed in the Expert groups. The large concept map must start with the descriptor NUTRIENTS.

   Provide additional descriptors to connect the Expert group maps to the large map. You may change the maps from the Expert groups any way that you wish. The final map must appear to be a single entity, not just a gluing-together of the individual parts. You may add special touches to make your group's map unique and different from those of the other groups.

   Draw the final copy of your concept map on the large sheet of paper provided. Hand this copy in. Each member of the group should also keep a copy. (30 min.)

Notes

Section 2
Plant Physiology

Student Activity 2.1 Seed Germination and Seedling Growth

Teacher Background

Introduction

In this laboratory, students experiment with fresh plant material using the "scroll method." Refer to the figure on the student page to see how the scrolls are set up. Students investigate the germination events of seeds and test various external factors on seed germination and seedling growth.

The author first became acquainted with the use of scrolls to examine factors affecting seed germination during the University of Guelph's UPDATE for Secondary Teachers, Feb. 1995. At that time, Denise McClellan, a lab technician working in the lab of Dr. W.E. Rauser, presented a session entitled "Growing Plants that Work in the Classroom," where the scrolls were used.

Advantages of Using Scrolls

1. Easy to teach to students and for students to manipulate.
2. Economical:
   · cost of materials: no pots or soil
   · space: many seedlings per scroll
   · minimal care: can leave over weekends
   · minimal time to prepare for students
   · supplies readily available: reusable containers
3. Clean: no messy soil, clean-up of containers.
4. Accumulate lots of data readily: could have up to 10 seedlings per scroll.
5. Reproducible.
6. May observe entire plant during experimental process. (Towels can be separated and reset).
7. May be used to carry out a variety of experiments.

Teaching Notes

_____

_____

_____

_____

_____

_____

_____

_____

_____

_____

_____

_____

_____

_____

Student Activity 2.1 Seed Germination and Seedling Growth

Purpose

To study a variety of factors which affect seed germination and the growth of seedlings.

Materials

seeds (corn, pea, bean, others)
forceps
ruler
spray bottle
container that allows light penetration
masking tape
plant hormones (optional)
salt solutions (optional)
pH solutions (optional)
paper towels (folded, brown commercial-type)
light source
water

Possible Experiments

The experimental setup, using scrolls, can be applied to the study of a number of different experiments. Some possible studies are as follows:

1. Developmental study of corn and soybean seedlings over time (e.g., for seven days).
2. Comparison of different types of seeds: sunflower, bean, pea, corn, cucumber, barley, rice, soybean, etc.
3. Examination of stages of seed germination.
4. Gravitropism in corn seedling growth.
5. Salt stress in corn and barley. (Try using $CaCl_2$ road salt.)
6. Growth regulation in seedling germination (gibberellins or auxins).
7. Phototropism in seedling growth (positioning of light source).
8. Variation of light quality using colored filters, or by varying the intensity or duration of light.
9. Effect(s) of pH on growth. Dip towels in solutions of different pH (consequences of acid precipitation, irrigation, fertilizer runoff).
10. Nodulation in legumes. *Rhizobium* sp. is available at farm supply stores or seed companies.

Method for Scrolls

1. Collect seeds, paper towels, masking tape, ruler, containers, water.
2. Wet one paper towel and lay it on a flat surface.
3. Place seeds in a row, about 1.5 cm from the top folded edge and at least 2 cm from the outside edges. Orient seeds as desired.
4. Wet another paper towel and lay evenly over the first towel and seeds.
5. Starting from the outside edge, roll the towels into a scroll with internal diameter of about 4 cm (maintain this size — too small creates anoxic conditions).
6. Stand the scroll upright with the folded edge and seeds at the top, and allow excess water to drain for 1-2 min.
7. Place the scroll upright in a container, cover with a lid (e.g., another cup), and tape securely in place.
8. Place in a growing area and monitor moisture levels as needed.

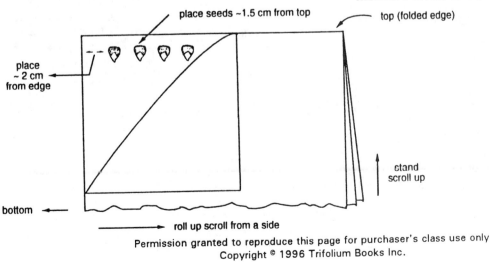

place seeds ~1.5 cm from top

top (folded edge)

place ~ 2 cm from edge

stand scroll up

bottom

roll up scroll from a side

Student Activity 2.2
The Action of Bromelin and Papain on Gelatin

Introduction

Enzymes or their preparations from certain tropical plants can be used in the laboratory to demonstrate proteolytic activity. Examples include papain from the latex of the papaya plant and bromelin from pineapples.

When dissolved in water, gelatin forms a semi-solid, 3-dimensional protein network which traps large amounts of water. When the protein network is broken down by proteolytic enzymes, the water is released and the gelatin liquifies. For this experiment, a suitable substrate is Knox gelatin, commercially available as dehydrated powders.

Purpose

To examine the proteolytic action of bromelin and papain on rehydrated gelatin at room temperature.

Note: Temperature conditions may be varied, e.g., low temperature (0-5°C), metabolic temperature (37-40°C), hot (45-50°C), and boiling (100°C).

Materials

gelatin (Knox)
balance
distilled water
measuring cylinders
2 beakers
stirring rod
bunsen burner
tripod with wire gauze
small Petri dishes
fresh pineapple (bromelin source)
food processor
meat tenderizer, Adolph's (papain source)
grease pencil or marker
toothpicks

Method

1. Preparation of the gelatin gel: add 6 g Knox gelatin to 100 mL distilled water in a beaker. Heat gently until the gelatin powder dissolves completely. Pour the resulting mixture into clean petri dishes to a depth of 5 mm. Store in a refrigerator until required for use in class. **Note:** Make sure that the gelatin is at room temperature before using it. Remove the dishes from the refrigerator about 2 h before use.
2. Preparation of the bromelin source: blend two slices of a freshly peeled pineapple (50 g approx.) in a food processor for 1 min. Decant the mixture into a beaker.
3. Label three Petri dishes containing gelatin: O = no enzymes, distilled water only; B = bromelin source, blended pineapple; and P = papain source, meat tenderizer.
4. Addition of the enzyme sources: Add distilled water, blended pineapple, or meat tenderizer to the appropriate Petri dishes. Add just enough to cover the gelatin surface.
5. Evaluating the gelatin for proteolysis: Initially and at 5-min intervals, gently poke the gelatin surfaces using the blunt end of a toothpick. Look for evidence of gel liquefaction (as an index of proteolysis). Record your observations. Continue your observations for 15 min.

Observations

Use a scale from 1-3 to record enzyme proteolytic action in the Observations Chart on the following page.
1 = no liquefaction or change in texture.
2 = slight gelatin liquefaction.
3 = most gelatin liquefaction.

Discussion

1. In which plate did the gelatin liquefaction first occur?
2. Protein can be hydrolyzed by enzymatic action. What does hydrolyzed mean?
3. a. When proteins are hydrolyzed, amino acids and another compound are produced. What is this other compound?
   b. Where does this other compound come from?
   c. Explain the enzymatic liquefaction of gelatin observed in this experiment.

4. Explain what you observed in dish O.
5. When making a jellied fruit salad, should you use fresh or canned pineapple slices? Give reasons for your choice.
6. Design an experiment to determine the effect of temperature on the proteolytic activity of one of the enzymes used in the present experiment. Which enzyme would you use? Why?

Observations Chart

1 = no liquefaction or change in texture.
2 = slight gelatin liquefaction.
3 = most gelatin liquefaction.

Petri dish	Enzyme Proteolytic Score			
	Time (min)			
	0	5	10	15
O				
B				
P				

Student Activity 2.3 The Green Thumb Mystery!!

Teacher Background

This activity is designed to be used as a review exercise for a Senior Biology unit on Photosynthesis. Students must use their knowledge of photosystems I and II to solve the crime.

At the completion of the activity, students should be able to:

• indicate that the presence of Atrazine blocks the acceptance of electrons by quinone in Photosystem I.

(a) This blockage inhibits the entire movement of electrons, resulting in no production of $NADPH_2$.
(b) The absence of this molecule prevents the Calvin cycle from producing glucose.
(c) Ultimately the plant dies when it runs out of glucose.

Teaching Notes

You may wish to record student responses to their "Mission" here, for future assessment ideas and/or for assistance to students who may need more help.

_____

_____

_____

_____

_____

_____

_____

_____

_____

_____

_____

_____

_____

_____

_____

_____

_____

_____

_____

_____

Student Activity 2.3 **The Green Thumb Mystery!!**

Last summer, the following report was filed by the investigating officer at the murder scene of a Ms. Dandy Lion. The victim was wilted and pale in color. It appeared as if she had suffered a severe case of glucose deprivation. The following statements were given to the police officer by members of the chloroplast.

Your Mission

1. Illustrate the crime scene, indicating where all of the witnesses were located and what they were doing.
2. Conduct a background investigation on Herb E. Cide, alias Atrazine. Summarize his personality traits.
3. Outline, in order, the steps that lead to the untimely death of Ms. Dandy Lion and identify the guilty party. Substantiate your accusation.

P680: I was hanging out, as usual, in the thylakoid membrane, receiving packets of energy from the radiant source.

QUINONE: P700 kept sending me those high energy electrons. As usual I would pick them up and lower them down the sequence of cytochromes.

WATER: P680 was noted for getting unstable and ejecting an electron. That always shook things up around here, causing a couple of my friends to split. The resulting electron always entered the thylakoid membrane, heading over to fill in at P680.

ELECTRONS: We stopped in at the thylakoid membrane, expecting to see a vacancy, but when we got there everything was full. There was no room to wait around.

FERRODOXIN: I heard from a passing electron that Herb E. Cide had been seen heading over toward Photosystem I.

P700: I had just sent out one of our energized electrons, expecting a replacement from Photosystem II at any time. Nobody showed.

NADP: I usually hooked up with a couple of electrons and H ions and headed over to the Calvin Cycle to help make some glucose. Everyone knows we can't get by without good old glucose. The electrons didn't show up and I couldn't go alone. Next thing I knew everything was shutting down.

CYTOCHROMES: (Photosystem I) Give me an electron, I pass it on. I can't pass what I don't have!

HERB E. CIDE was not available for questioning. It has been reported that he likes to move in and take over for electrons.

Section 3
Animal Physiology

Teacher Activity 3.1 A Blood Concept Map

You may use this concept map as an overhead, as a handout, or as part of a test (with certain parts deleted).

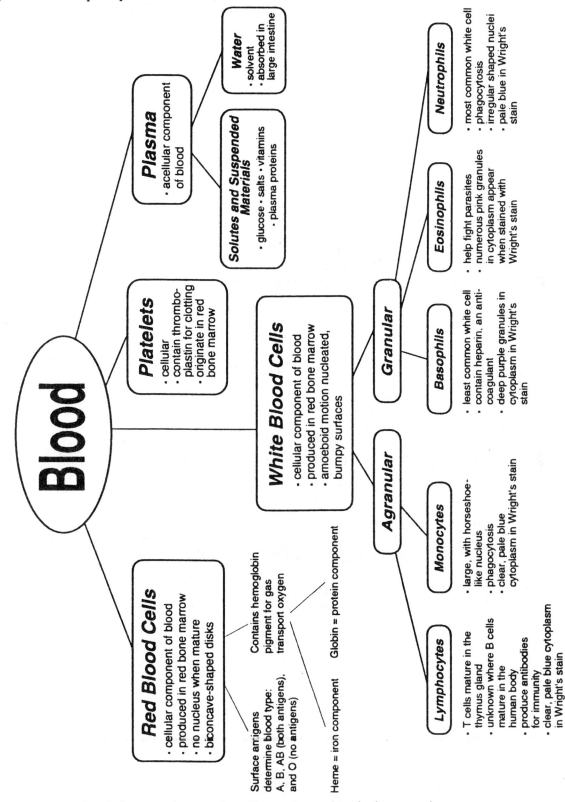

Student Activity 3.2 A Sherlock Holmes Who Done It?
The Case of Comparative Anatomy

Teacher Background

The Mystery

This activity is designed to encourage students to use their knowledge of the taxonomy, anatomy, and physiology of organisms to solve a mystery. Note that the students do not know at the outset whether or not the Vet has been murdered or has succumbed to an illness. As the plot unfolds, this should become apparent. The clues and the interpretation which might be applied to each are as follows (if your students are lacking the background in any aspect of the case, please provide additional clues as needed):

CLUE 1 - PIG - This vertebrate is a common source of insulin.

CLUE 2 - CAT (or another fur bearing creature) - The hair, although not a real clue, implicates a fur-bearing creature in the crime.

CLUE 3 - HUMAN - The human is the only organism depicted which exhibits bipedal locomotion.

CLUE 4 - CATS - Cats have a 3:1:3:1 dentition pattern above, and 3:1:2:1 below.

CLUE 5 - HUMAN - the one who wanted the Vet dead, and CAT, the reason(???). This is perhaps not yet apparent!

CLUE 6 - HUMAN - The reference here is to human (unsuccessful at murdering the victim), and to the fact that the center of mass moved forward over evolutionary time to a more vertical stance.

CLUE 7 - RABBIT - The rabbit has the least developed stereoscopic vision of the organisms listed.

CLUE 8 - A RABID RABBIT - A rabid rabbit appears to be the caused of death.

Solution

In the final analysis, it appears that the restaurant was serving cat meat and rabbit meat to the unknowing patrons. The owner of the restaurant would have good reason for keeping the VET quiet because a disclosure that cat meat was being served would ruin his business. However, the consumption of the meat from the rabid rabbit achieved that end before the owner could.

This is a biology activity but it raises a couple of legal points for you to consider. Should the owner of the restaurant be charged, if not with murder, then with criminal negligence causing the death? Some food for legal thought!

Teaching Notes

_____

_____

_____

_____

_____

_____

_____

_____

Student Activity 3.2 A Sherlock Holmes Who Done It?
The Case of Comparative Anatomy

The Mystery

A former veterinarian had found himself in a bit of "hot water" with a private supplier of cats and rabbits to the university. In an attempt to relax his troubled and somewhat nervous state, he made his way to Bio 101 Cafe - his favorite restaurant. There, horror of horrors, he met an untimely death. What could have caused this tragedy? Why would someone want him dead? Was his death something which had been planned or was it simply an accident? One or more of the vertebrates which appear in the accompanying figure are implicated in the death. Use your knowledge of anatomy and physiology to solve the mystery.

For each of the clues that follow, try to identify the vertebrate(s) involved with the specific clue. Use these clues to eliminate a suspect or to build a case to solve the mystery.

In summary, how did the Vet meet his death? Who wanted him killed and what was the motive? And finally, were these one and the same?

Extention

Produce a mystery to solve yourself that requires scientific knowledge in order to solve it. Try it out on your classmates - to help them review material or as a self-test.

The Clues

CLUE 1 - In talking to the Vet's co-workers, Sherlock finds that the Vet was insulin-dependent. Name the animal in the above figures which is common source of insulin. Sherlock requests that you eliminate this suspect from the list of potential killers for reasons he cannot disclose at this time.

CLUE 2 - Watson, Sherlock's partner, goes to the Bio 101 Cafe where the Vet died and finds a small bit of fur near the table where the Vet had been sitting. Assume that this fur gives him a clue as to the motive behind the crime.

CLUE 3 - Sherlock decides that he would like to scour the little restaurant for additional clues himself. Much to his surprise he was quite astonished to find how dirty the place had been kept. The floor was sticky from a spilled container of catsup. But this turned to be advantageous for the clever Sherlock. What he found was another possible clue: footprints. He was told by one of the clients of the restaurant that this animal exhibited bipedal locomotion. Sherlock wrote this clue in his memo pad as a clue to the one who wanted to kill the Vet.

CLUE 4 - It was Watson's turn to visit the restaurant and he wasn't very pleased in what he was assigned. Sherlock requested that Watson pick through the garbage, searching for more clues. Watson's mood made a complete change when his adventure in the garbage picking turned out to be quite rewarding. In the garbage he found several skulls that exhibited a dentation pattern of 3:1:3:1 above and 3:1:2:1 below, unlike the 2:1:2:3 pattern of human beings. Sherlock looked over Watson's report and wrote a note to himself that read, "another hint as to why someone might want our poor Vet DEAD!

CLUE 5 - In order to gain an inside edge and to show Sherlock how innovative he was, Watson decided to consult a Soothsayer. This Soothsayer had quite a good reputation with the police force. The police only consulted her when they were desperate and had no clues for a case. Apparently she was able to get information by reading auras. This is the clue that she gave Watson,

" The one who wanted to kill the Vet and the 'reason' for the crime both belong to the Class Mammalia. However, the one who wanted to kill the Vet belongs to the Order Primate and the 'reason' why the Vet would be killed had something to do with the Order Carnivora."

CLUE 6 - Unknown to Watson, a few days later Sherlock also consulted this same Soothsayer. The Soothsayer was very happy that Sherlock had dropped in because she felt that she had been getting stronger vibes today. She said that her auras told her that the one who wanted to kill the Vet was unsuccessful. The unsuccessful would-be killer had this characteristic: over the course of evolution, the center of mass of this creature moved from being forward back, until the organism stood erect over time.

CLUE 7 - Sherlock met a very frightened Watson back at his office. Apparently someone had left a note written in blood pinned to Sherlock's chair. The note read: "What killed the Vet is none other than the one with the least developed stereoscopic vision among the suspects!"

CLUE 8 - With this last tip, Sherlock and Watson marched off to the Bio 101 Cafe, determined to put "solved" to this case. In their final visit to the restaurant Sherlock and Watson interviewed two customers who had also been at the restaurant the night the Vet died. From these patrons they discovered that the Vet behaved strangely before dying. He was choking, had trouble swallowing liquids, and finally went into convulsions before dying.

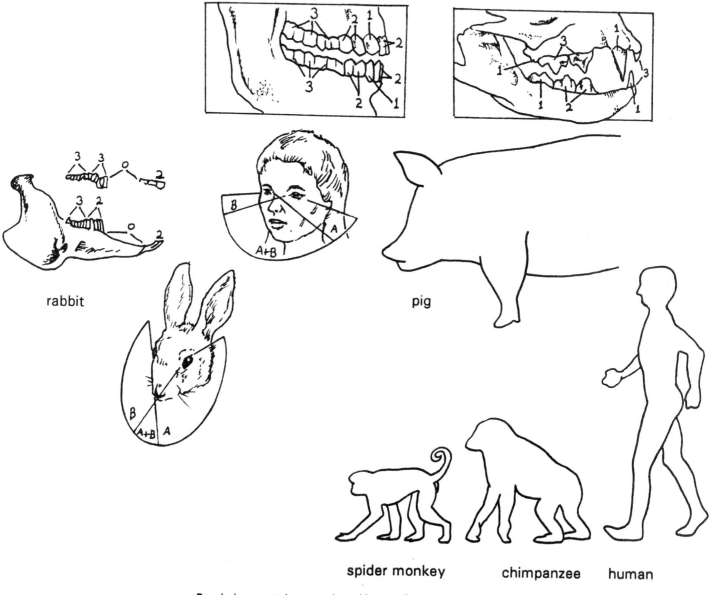

human

cat

rabbit

pig

spider monkey   chimpanzee   human

Student Activity 3.3 The Control of Breathing

Teacher Background

Introduction

When students begin to learn about the transport and exchange of gases, they often simply attempt to memorize the concentration gradients in order to remember the mechanics of breathing. They may remember it better if they have an understanding of the control of breathing by the nervous system, and the important role that carbon dioxide plays in stimulating breathing. The carbon dioxide level in the blood passing through the brain is monitored by the respiratory control center in the central nervous system.

Airport Scenario

It is also important for students to understand that although breathing normally has a regular rhythm, the respiratory control center can sometimes change that rhythm based on other information it receives from the body. Hyperventilation is a good example of the system being altered, and the paper bag remedy reinforces the importance of carbon dioxide in the control of the breathing process.

The following scenario suggests an increased heart and breathing rate. The students must think about the gas exchange occurring, the message that the nervous system would be receiving about the CO_2 and O_2 levels, and lastly, the gas collecting in the paper bag, in order to explain hyperventilation, the factors leading to its occurrence, and its treatment.

Teaching Notes

_____

_____

_____

_____

_____

_____

_____

_____

_____

_____

_____

_____

_____

_____

_____

_____

_____

_____

_____

Student Activity 3.3 **The Control of Breathing**

Scene: A Major Airport

Anika stands in the check-in line at the airport. She's finally going to visit her cousins in Trinidad. She's excited. Once again she makes sure she has her ticket, her passport, all the necessary documents. She looks around, and the young woman in the line beside her smiles. They begin a conversation. Anika discovers that the young woman's name is Danielle, it's her first trip anywhere outside of Canada, and she's also excited. Anika and Danielle continue to chat while they wait. Anika notices that Danielle is sweating a great deal, even though the airport is air-conditioned.

"Are you okay?" asks Anika.

"Well, I'm a little nervous," replies Danielle.

"Don't worry. Let's get seats together, and I'll keep you company on the plane."

"Thanks, that would be great!" exclaims Danielle.

As they get closer to the counter, Anika notices that Danielle is breathing faster and louder. Then, she says she can't catch her breath. Anika asks the next person in line to watch Danielle and she runs off to a nearby book store. She returns with a paper bag, shakes it out and places it over Danielle's nose and mouth, holding it tightly. Within a few minutes, Danielle's breathing rate has slowed down and she begins to feel better.

Your Mission

Explain what happened, and how Anika's actions helped Danielle.

Notes

_____

_____

_____

_____

_____

_____

_____

_____

_____

_____

_____

_____

_____

_____

_____

_____

_____

_____

Student Activity 3.4 Designing a Circulatory System

Teacher Background

Introduction

In this activity, students decide on the functions of a circulatory system and design a structure to fit its functions.

You might decide to begin an animal physiology unit with circulation, instead of nutrition, digestion, respiration, or excretion, so you can see if these related functions are included in the students' designs. This activity could serve as an introduction to the chapter on circulation, to determine what students already know, what misconceptions they might have, etc. Alternatively, use it at the end of the chapter to sum up the students' knowledge of the function of a circulatory system.

Procedure

1. Organize students into groups of 2 to 4 and give them a sheet of newsprint, some markers, and one period in which to do this activity.
2. Do not permit students to refer to their textbooks during the activity.
3. You may wish to ask the question "How would you design a circulatory system so that all body parts receive the same materials"?
4. Models would be left with the teacher and students could explain them to the class in the following period.

Assessment

If a mark is to be assigned, or if you use either self- or peer-assessment of an activity, use a scheme such as the following:

	0	1	2	3	4	5
Parts labelled	0	1	2	3		
Functions described	0	1	2	3	4	5
Direction of transport shown		1	2			
Creativity in design	0	1	2			
Overall completeness	0	1	2	3		

Total: /15

Student Activity 3.4 Designing a Circulatory System

Introduction

Challenge yourselves to design a circulatory system. You can produce a design based on what you know about a real system, such as a mammal, or you can "make up" both the animal and its system. As long as your design performs all the functions of a circulatory system, your animal may be real or fictitious. Don't forget that many animals have circulatory systems that are less complex than a mammal's system, yet these animals are very successful (insects, for example).

Your Instructions

Produce a two-dimensional model of a circulatory system of a real or fictitious animal. In doing so, consider the following questions:

1. What functions does a circulatory system serve in the body?
2. What is a circulatory system connected to?
3. How is it connected?

Your design must show:
(a) labelled parts or legend (use general terms)
(b) labels/symbols indicating the functions of different parts (be brief).
(c) arrows indicating the direction of transport.

Design Notes

_____

_____

_____

_____

_____

_____

_____

_____

_____

_____

_____

_____

_____

_____

_____

_____

_____

Student Activity 3.5
Vertebrate Gas Exchange: Role-Playing Exercise

Teacher Background

Introduction

The following exercise is designed to be used in a Vertebrate Gas-Exchange Systems Unit. It could be used at the beginning of the unit to stimulate interest and help prepare the students for material to be covered. Or, it could be used at the end of the unit as a review of the material.

The activity would be assigned prior to the date of the performance (role playing). You might give students a period of class time in which to prepare for the role playing. The actual role playing (performances) require at least two periods, one of which should be 75 min in length. These periods should probably not be sequential because you should inform the students of their success in the first role-playing exercise before they participate in the second exercise.

Problems

The method for this activity could be used to present any of the concepts listed below.
1. Explain how the structure of each part of the gas-exchange system examined is suited to its function.
2. Describe the physical principles and mechanisms of human inspiration and expiration.
3. Explain how oxygen and carbon dioxide are transported in humans.
4. Describe the path of an oxygen molecule as it travels from the nasal cavity to an internal cell of a human (e.g., cell of the gall bladder).

Lesson/Day 1

Students are given the assignment sheets in class. You may choose to give them some class time in which to prepare for the role-playing exercise.
1. Students are given the following list of terms: epiglottis, trachea, bronchus (bronchi), bronchioles, alveolus (alveoli), diaphragm, pulmonary capillary (capillaries), pleura, rib cage (intercostal muscles of rib cage), hemoglobin, oxygen, carbon dioxide, bicarbonate ion, red blood cell(s), diffusion, nasal cavity, cilia, mucus, macrophage(s), pharynx, larynx, glottis, and blood plasma (23 terms).

2. Tell students that they will be taking part in a role-playing exercise on vertebrate gas exchange systems in which they must assume the role of one of the terms listed.

3. For each term, have every student write statements that describe the structure and function of the term as it relates to:
   a. the physical principles and mechanisms of human inspiration and expiration (i.e., describe the processes of inspiration and expiration);
   b. the transportation of oxygen and carbon dioxide in humans;
   c. tracing the path of an oxygen molecule from the nasal cavity to an internal cell of a human.

Students may NOT use the actual term in their description. For example, a student might use the following sentences if writing about the term "cell wall."

I support and protect a plant cell.
I am frequently made of cellulose.
I am not found in animal cells.

Lesson/Day 2

4. On the agreed date, the students in turn select a term or process from a "hat" at the front of the room. They then print their names and the name of their terms on your mark sheet. The papers with the term on it are given back to you, and the performer must NOT discuss their term with any other student. Each student is given five minutes in which to prepare and give a performance illustrating the term. They may read or act out their terms, using their prepared descriptions if desired. At your discretion, the student may use any props present in the classroom.

All students do NOT select their terms at the same time. Instead, the first student selects and performs a term while the rest of the class "judges" the performance.

5. While a student is performing, the other students in the class write the name of the performer and what term they think the performer represents. Students MUST use ink to write this. Students may NOT cross out any answer or use "white out." Once a student writes an answer, it is permanent.

6. As the student is performing, grade each student on:

	Poor/Adequate/Good
Accuracy of their description	1 3 5
Creativity or humor	1 3 5

7. Once all students have performed, read out the terms that each student selected. All members of the class write (in INK) the correct terms on their sheet.

8. Ask for a show of hands for correct identification of each term. The percentage of students that correctly identify a term from the role-playing exercise is used to generate a mark for the performer.

	Marks
100% of the class guessed correctly	10
86-99% of the class guessed correctly	9
76-85% of the class guessed correctly	8
64-75% of the class guessed correctly	7
60-65% of the class guessed correctly	6
55-59% of the class guessed correctly	5
less than 55% of the class guessed correctly	4

9. As a check, collect the sheets from each student at the end of the class.

10. Depending on time constraints and whether or not all members of the class were able to role play, you may choose to continue the exercise for more than one period.

Lesson/Day 3

This could occur up to a week after the initial role-playing activity. It should NOT occur until after you return the marks for the first role-playing exercise to the students.

11. Students are responsible for performing the term that they chose in the earlier role-playing exercise. Students may bring ONE cue card containing any information on their term that they feel may be necessary for this exercise.

12. Choose one of the following processes or descriptions:
    a. inspiration
    b. expiration
    c. transportation of oxygen in humans
    d. transportation of carbon dioxide in humans
    e. tracing the path of an oxygen molecule as it travels from the nasal cavity to an internal cell of a human body (give an example of an internal cell)

13. The class is given ten to fifteen minutes to brainstorm and organize themselves to describe the process or description. Students will then perform/role play the terms they selected from the previous role-playing assignment.

14. The class role plays the various structures and processes necessary for the process or description to occur. Students may use cue cards for their performance.

15. Mark the class on the process or description in terms of:
    a. Were all the necessary structures/processes included? Total of 10 marks (minus 0.5 for each omission).
    b. Were all the structures and processes performed in their correct order? Total of 10 marks (minus 0.5 mark for each error).
    c. Were all the terms used correctly in causing the process to occur? Total of 10 marks (minus 1 mark for each error).

16. You may choose to ask the class to role play another process or description.

Student Activity 3.5
Vertebrate Gas Exchange: Role-Playing Exercise

1. Study the following terms: epiglottis, trachea, bronchus (bronchi), bronchioles, alveolus (alveoli), diaphragm, pulmonary capillary (capillaries), pleura, rib cage (intercostal muscles of rib cage), hemoglobin, oxygen, carbon dioxide, bicarbonate ion, red blood cell(s), diffusion, nasal cavity, cilia, mucus, macrophage(s), pharynx, larynx, glottis, and blood plasma.

2. Research the structure and function of each term and write two or three statements for each term that precisely and accurately describe the structure and function of the term. You will be required to assume the role of one of the terms listed above and you may use your descriptions of the term in your performance. Take special care in constructing your descriptions. You may NOT use the name of the term in either your descriptions or your performance.

   For example, if you had chosen the term "cell wall," you might use the following descriptions:

   I support and protect a plant cell.
   I am frequently made of cellulose.
   I am not found in animal cells.

3. The role-playing exercise may involve two components and take two class periods. During the first period, you will randomly select a term and assume the role of that term in front of the class.

   During the second period, the class will work together to demonstrate/describe one or more of the following:
   a. the physical principles and mechanisms of human inspiration and expiration (i.e., describe the processes of inspiration and expiration);
   b. the transportation of oxygen and carbon dioxide in humans;
   c. the path of an oxygen molecule from the nasal cavity to an internal cell of a human.

4. On the day assigned, bring your descriptions of ALL the terms to class plus a pen that writes in INK. Each student then randomly selects a term and has a maximum of five

minutes to prepare and perform the term. You may choose to read your description or to act out the term. With the teacher's permission, props from within the class may be used.
   * Your performance will be graded by your teacher on the basis of accuracy of your description and creativity or humor.
   * You will also be graded on how well the class figures out what term you represent.

5. Your teacher will return the marks to each student.

6. On a later date, the entire class may do the second role-playing exercise. You will assume the same role as in the first exercise. You may prepare and bring ONE cue card that contains any information on your term that you think is necessary for your performance.

7. The teacher will select one (or more) of the following processes/descriptions:
   a. inspiration
   b. expiration
   c. transportation of oxygen in humans
   d. transportation of carbon dioxide in humans
   e. tracing the path of an oxygen molecule as it travels from the nasal cavity to an internal cell of a human body.

8. Your class will have ten to fifteen minutes to brainstorm and organize yourselves to describe the process or description. You may use cue cards for your performances.

9. The teacher will mark the class on the process or description in terms of:
   a. Were all the necessary structures/ processes included? Total of 10 marks (minus 0.5 for each omission).
   b. Were all the structures and processes performed in their correct order? Total of 10 marks (minus 0.5 mark for each error).
   c. Were all the terms used correctly in causing the process to occur? Total of 10 marks (minus 1 mark for each error).

Student Activity 3.6 Digestion within a Chocolate Covered Cherry

Teacher Background

The chocolate covered cherry model activity may be used in the senior biology unit on the chemical basis of life. It relates enzyme activity to an organism's digestive processes. Students explore the properties of complex and simple sugars and the relationships between them. They can relate this to the ease of absorption of monosaccharides versus di- and polysaccharides, thus indicating the necessity of complete chemical digestion.

Students will have an opportunity to investigate an enzyme system found in an everyday product, and to problem-solve collaboratively by examining the enzymatic catabolism of sugars.

Assessment

List of ingredients	0	1					
List of enzymes	0	1	2				
List of substrate(s)/product(s)	0	1	2				
Table completion	0	1	2	3	4	5	6
Enzyme substrate interaction	0	1	2				
Relate model to human digestion	0	1	2				
Total		/15					

Teaching Notes

_____

_____

_____

_____

_____

_____

_____

_____

_____

_____

_____

_____

_____

Student Activity 3.6 Digestion within a Chocolate Covered Cherry

Purpose
Identify the enzyme activity in the center of a chocolate covered cherry.

Materials
An empty chocolate covered cherry box or wrapper.

Think Pair-Share Learning Strategy
Your teacher will give you a period of time to think about your own answers to Instructions 1-6. Then pair off with a partner and discuss your answers, trying your best to agree on answers. Everyone will then be brought back together to share answers with the entire class.

Instructions
Think, pair, and share.
1. List the ingredients.
2. Identify the enzyme(s).
3. Identify the substrate(s) and product(s).
4. Construct a table comparing the following properties of the substrate(s) and product(s): formula, structural diagram, and solubility.
5. Relate the enzyme-substrate interaction to the nature of the chocolate covered cherry filling (not including the cherry).
6. Relate the chocolate covered cherry model to the digestion of carbohydrates within humans.

Teaching Notes

_____

_____

_____

_____

_____

_____

_____

_____

_____

_____

_____

_____

_____

_____

_____

_____

Teacher Activity 3.7 Transport in Animals and Plants

Problem

Many textbooks treat transport in animals separately from transport in plants. Often, little or no emphasis is made on the similarities in the principles involved and the function(s) achieved. Here is a novel approach to this topic.

Begin by getting students to suggest the overall significance of transport, working either individually or in groups. Illustrative examples should be supplied from mammals, other animals, and plants. The students could then be given the following table with only the headings included. Their task is to compare the transport systems found in animals and plants.

Differences

In the course of the lesson, emphasize the following differences:

1. The main tissues involved:
   Vertebrate animals: heart, muscular and epithelial (blood vessels). Compare invertebrate transport systems (where found) with vertebrate systems.
   plants: xylem, phloem sieve tubes.
2. Plants have no pumping mechanism which can be compared with the vertebrate heart.
3. The vertebrate blood vessels are living whereas the mature xylem are dead cells that form hollow tubes.
4. Plants have no organ similar to the vertebrate lungs or gills; however, the leaves (e.g., mesophyte) provide large surface areas for the diffusion of gases.
5. In plants, transpiration facilitates the upward movement of water. Perspiration occurs in some vertebrates, but this process does not significantly affect fluid (blood) transport.
6. Plants wilt when the transpiration rate exceeds the water absorption rate. In contrast, vertebrates drink to satisfy their need for water. When water intake is low, excretion via the kidneys may be reduced as a compensatory mechanism.

Related Lab Exercises

Activities may include:
measuring blood pressure and pulse rate;
measuring transpiration rate;
examining the structure of the heart (fresh specimens and/or models);
examining prepared microscope slides to study the structure of the heart and blood vessels;
examining roots, stems, and leaves microscopically to observe xylem and phloem.

Assessment

Quizzes, tests, and other assignments may stress the similarities in function while recognizing structural differences.

Concept	Mammals	Plants
Fluid	Blood	Sap
System	Blood system consists of: - heart (muscular pump) - arteries take blood to the tissues - veins return blood to the heart - capillaries form connecting links in the tissues between arterioles and venules, and are involved in nutrient and gas exchange with the cells	Vascular system forms a continuous pipeline connecting the roots, stems, and leaves. It consists of: - xylem (water and mineral transport: cohesion-tension hypothesis) - phloem sieve tubes (transport of dissolved materials: pressure flow hypothesis)
Pressure	Blood pressure can be measured. Osmotic pressure of the blood can be determined.	Root pressure, osmotic pressure, and transpiration rate can be measured in actively growing plants. Useful illustrations from your textbooks would include diagrams of the circulatory system in a vertebrate and of vascular tissue in plants.

Teacher Activity 3.7 (continued)

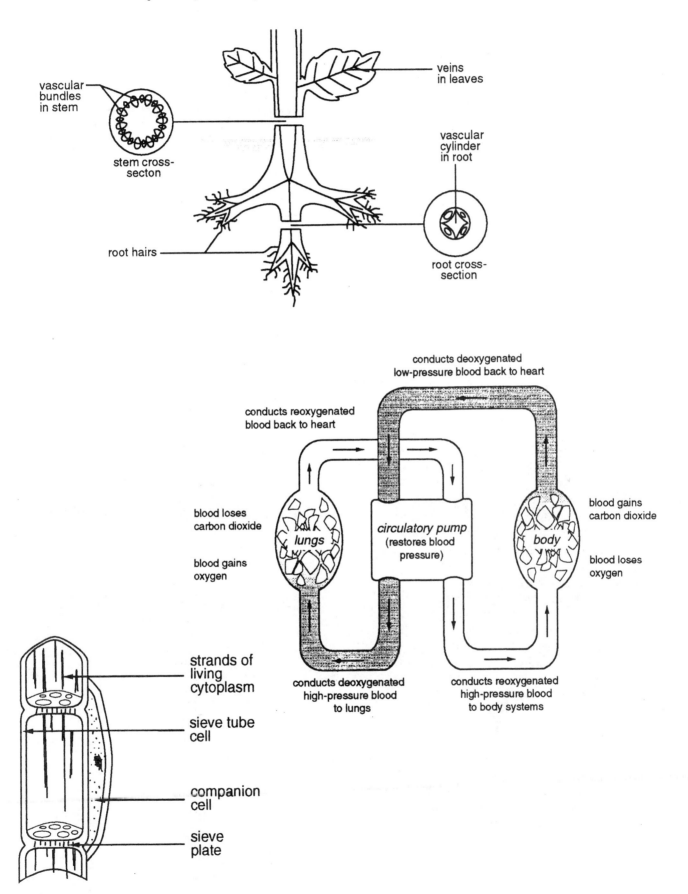

vascular bundles in stem

stem cross-secton

veins in leaves

vascular cylinder in root

root hairs

root cross-section

conducts deoxygenated low-pressure blood back to heart

conducts reoxygenated blood back to heart

blood loses carbon dioxide

lungs

blood gains oxygen

circulatory pump (restores blood pressure)

blood gains carbon dioxide

body

blood loses oxygen

conducts deoxygenated high-pressure blood to lungs

conducts reoxygenated high-pressure blood to body systems

strands of living cytoplasm

sieve tube cell

companion cell

sieve plate

Student Activity 3.8 Case Studies in Human Physiology

Teacher Background

When studying the systems of the human body, many curriculum units suggest extension activities dealing with aspects of diseases or disorders in these systems. A successful way of incorporating an examination of health issues is the introduction of case studies. The accompanying case studies may be used at the end of the respiratory system unit or a circulatory system unit, or as a synthesis for both units. The cases themselves are brief. Some groups may take unique and unexpected angles to their case studies.

Procedure

1. Give the students the case only. Cut the clues off and set them aside for students who choose to use them.
2. The case studies may be photocopied on different colors of paper. Students with the same colored paper can then easily group themselves into jigsaw research groups which will research the same case.
3. After the cases have been handed out and the students are in their research groups, give the class time to brainstorm. Each student will brainstorm individually for two minutes before group brainstorming begins.
4. Circulate among the groups in order to monitor the direction each group is taking in its approach to the problem, and also to be on hand to clarify aspects of the case or brainstorming questions.
5. Let students know that clues (questions outlining possible approaches) are available for each case study. However, groups choosing to use the clues forfeit a tenth of the total mark value (i.e., 5/50). With careful brainstorming and concept mapping, groups should not have to resort to asking for the clues.
6. Have each group draw a concept map which it must discuss with you before library research begins. This gives the students an opportunity to explain their approach or "plan of attack" before starting research. Students should hand in their rough notes to show their individual contributions to the group's work.
7. Hold research days in the lab and library.

8. Each research group hands in the brainstorm concept map, a final report, and a bibliography or reference list. The jigsaw is completed on a discussion day when the research groups disband and discussion groups form (one member from each research group). In this application of the jigsaw technique, the research is emphasized more than the presentation. The discussion groups are often more of a forum for the exchange of ideas and findings between the students from different research groups rather than a more formal seminar in which students teach their peers about their topic.
9. If the researched information is crucial to the curriculum, then each research group could provide a summary sheet which can be photocopied and given to each student in the seminar or presentation group. This summary sheet would also be handed in for evaluation, and the overall evaluation could also include peer- or self-evaluations.

Case studies motivate the students by injecting a dose of real life into the course, and by allowing them to apply the brainstorming and problem-solving skills introduced earlier in their courses. It is also a time-effective way of covering a variety of interesting health concerns using active inquiry, and a good way to incorporate societal or ethical issues.

Student Activity 3.8 Case Studies in Human Physiology

Case 1

Craig is an 18-year-old with cystic fibrosis. Up until recently his condition has been fairly stable, despite a gradual decline in lung function. His childhood and youth were normal in all respects, except that he always had to stay relatively close to home because of his daily routine of treatment, including physical therapy and medicines. However, he has recently been accepted to a university in another part of the country in a competitive program with limited space. He desperately wants to go, but his family is worried. They feel that he hasn't thought through the practical aspects of moving away, such as his treatment routine, and the fact that his condition continues to deteriorate. Remaining close to home also means remaining close to his physician and the transplant registry (waiting list) he has been on since age fifteen. Realistically, what are Craig's options?

Case 2

Frank is a 45-year-old man who has smoked since age 14. Although not a chain smoker, he smokes moderately heavily. Recently at a family gathering he experienced a distressing episode of shortness of breath which was long enough and serious enough to warrant his admission to hospital. It turned out to be emphysema. This is not Frank's first complication resulting from smoking n he has had an annoying smoker's cough for years. His wife has constantly tried to get him to quit smoking, citing lung cancer and second-hand smoke effects as her main concerns. How serious is Frank's prognosis?

Case 3

Renee is a 32-year-old professional woman. Undergoing a routine physical examination and expressing no complaints, she is very surprised by her doctor's revelation that she has elevated blood pressure: 158/97. The doctor suggests, however, that this need not be cause for excessive worry as the lower number is not overly high — she would have greater cause for concern if the second number was higher than 110 mm Hg. Explaining to her doctor that she feels generally fine, Renee questions what might be the cause of this problem and what the complications might be if left untreated. What will the doctor tell her about her health and about lifestyle changes she might have to make?

Case 4

Philip, a 42-year-old architect who suffered a mild heart attack 17 months ago, is now scheduled to undergo his second balloon angioplasty since the attack. As his grandfather, uncle, and older brother all died from heart disease before the age of 45, he is very concerned about his future (or the lack of one). He also wants to prevent the need for any future surgery. His physician, however, suggests that although the problem has a strong genetic component which can't be altered, there are certain things that Philip can do to reduce the risk. Most of these are less risky and less costly than the bypass surgery performed immediately after his heart attack. What would be your advice to Philip?

Case 5

Mr. Granich, an 80-year-old retired teacher, desperately requires a heart transplant since the pacemaker embedded in his chest can no longer stimulate his diseased heart muscle. In the room down the hall lies Mr. Papastergiou, a 29-year-old biomedical researcher whose heart is barely functioning, having been ravaged by a viral infection which could be fatal within days if he does not receive a transplant. Tests conducted on both men indicate that they are both compatible with a donor heart which has just become available. What happens now?

Case 6

During her last visit to the doctor, Marie-Ange Dupuis was diagnosed with stenosis of the atrio-ventricular valves (tricuspid, bicuspid) which accounted for some of the symptoms she had been experiencing throughout the last year. Ultrasound imaging has just confirmed the doctor's diagnosis, so he is now discussing possible courses of action with Ms. Dupuis. Marie-Ange, however, is more concerned with the bulging knobs in the veins in her legs and the excruciating pain that makes standing and walking difficult. The doctor feels that the leg veins are not a priority and that they should deal with one health problem at a time. Which of the conditions do you think is serious enough to be the first priority?

Case 7

Jason, a five-year-old kindergarten pupil, has had a persistent rasping cough for weeks now. His teacher became concerned and contacted his parents. They told the teacher that they tried several commercial cough syrups without success. Several days after this conversation, the teacher notices that Jason's phlegm is often bloody. The school nurse examines Jason and suspects that the cough and unusual lung sounds might be symptoms of tuberculosis, a disease virtually unheard-of in this country today. The teacher notifies the principal, who feels that until the family's physician can independently confirm the diagnosis, Jason should remain in class. The situation has created a rift among the school staff, who are split in their opinions about what action to take. Your group must prepare a report for the staff and the principal, who will make a final decision based on your work.

Case 8

Marisa and John, a newlywed couple, are house hunting. They have focused mainly on older houses because they like the character and appeal of older homes. Also, they feel that the price range is better, and they could renovate the interior to their liking. Recently they found one home they love, but they have not made an offer on it because of one main factor: the house contains wall insulation and ceiling materials which are asbestos-based. John feels confident that the asbestos scare is overblown, but Marisa is concerned since her grandfather, a miner, died of asbestosis. Friends and family are split on the issue. Some fear the health risk of living in a home with asbestos, and others assure them that, if undisturbed or carefully handled, the risk is minimal. Should they allow this issue to stop them from buying this home?

CLUES FOR CASE 1

1. What are the causes, symptoms, and prognosis for cystic fibrosis?
2. How is it controlled or treated? What is involved in the daily life of C.F. patients: treatment routine, limitations, etc.?
3. What is involved in transplantation, such as linking donors and recipients, methods, success rates?

CLUES FOR CASE 2

1. Identify components of cigarette smoke and explain why they are dangerous.
2. Identify the symptoms, treatments, and prognosis for emphysema and lung cancer.
3. Discuss addiction and the difficulties faced by smokers in trying to quit. How successful are the various methods for quitting smoking?

CLUES FOR CASE 3

1. Define 158/97. What do these numbers normally represent?
2. Define hypertension, including different types and classifications and contributing factors.
3. Discuss possible complications of hypertension in the kidneys and in other blood vessels.
4. How is hypertension prevented, and how is it controlled?

CLUES FOR CASE 4

1. Discuss heart attack and atherosclerosis: their causes, prevalence, symptoms, and contributing factors.
2. Discuss treatments such as angioplasty and bypass surgery.
3. What are some of the social aspects of treatment: costs, shortage of beds, etc.?
4. What are some lifestyle changes recommended for people at risk for heart disease?

CLUES FOR CASE 5

1. Discuss initiation and control of heartbeat both normally and with artificial pacemakers.
2. Discuss viral and bacterial heart infections.
3. Investigate transplants: the methods, how donors and recipients are linked, and how organs are allocated. What are some of the ethical issues of transplant surgery?

CLUES FOR CASE 6

1. Define stenosis of the valves and its effects on normal heart function.
2. What is the treatment for stenosis? What is the possibility of valve replacement (real or artificial)?
3. Discuss varicose veins and their causes, symptoms, treatment, and prognosis.

CLUES FOR CASE 7

1. Define the causes and symptoms of tuberculosis. Include statistics on numbers of cases, mortality rates, etc.
2. Discuss prevention of the disease.
3. Discuss treatment methods for the disease.
4. How was tuberculosis virtually eradicated in this country?

CLUES FOR CASE 8

1. What is asbestos? Why is it so dangerous in the respiratory system?
2. What are the effects of asbestos in the respiratory system? Discuss the causes, symptoms, treatment, and prognosis for asbestosis.
3. What are some guidelines for the safe handling of asbestos?

Section 4
Homeostasis

Student Activity 4.1 Biology and Problem Solving
What Caused the Outbreak of Disease?

Teacher Background

Introduction

This problem-solving activity is based on an actual investigation into an epidemic of thyroid disease that occurred in Minnesota, South Dakota, and Iowa in 1984-85. The investigation revealed that the illness was caused by the consumption of ground beef that inadvertently contained pieces of cow thyroid tissue.

In this activity, students follow the epidemiological investigation that pinpointed that cause. Students are asked to develop hypotheses, set up an epidemiological study, and determine the cause of the outbreak in much the same way that the investigators did.

Background

Doctors investigating the disorder (known as thyrotoxicosis) described in this activity know that its usual cause is a malfunction of the immune system. In this condition, known as Grave's disease, antibodies are produced that stimulate the thyroid gland to secrete excess hormone.

Some other causes of thyrotoxicosis have been identified, including the ingestion of a thyroid preparation sold in health food stores as a dietary supplement, the consumption of pork sausage containing pig thyroid (this caused an epidemic in the 1960s), and the inflammation of the thyroid gland, sometimes caused by a virus.

As a result of the investigation described, the United States Department of Agriculture prohibited the use of livestock glands, as well as the muscle tissue surrounding the larynx, in meat prepared for human consumption.

Reference

Hedberg, C.W, et al. An outbreak of thyrotoxicosis caused by the consumption of bovine thyroid gland in ground beef. The New England Journal of Medicine (April 16, 1987): 993-99.

Procedure

You might like to give the information to the students in three parts: down to Question 2; the next paragraph plus Questions 3 and 4; and the last paragraph with Questions 5, 6, and 7. When the students (individually or in groups) have finished one part to your satisfaction, give them the next part.

Teaching Notes

_____

_____

_____

_____

_____

_____

_____

_____

_____

_____

_____

_____

_____

_____

Student Activity 4.1 Biology and Problem Solving
What Caused the Outbreak of Disease?

Case History

The patient's face was flushed. His heart was beating quickly, and he was short of breath. He complained of feeling restless and irritable. Results of blood tests showed a high level of thyroxine hormone in the bloodstream. This result was odd, because the patient's thyroid gland was not enlarged, as would have been expected.

Soon, other people who lived in the area showed similar symptoms. In all, over 1200 people in a nine-county area developed the same illness. What was causing such an outbreak?

To solve the mystery, doctors kept careful records of those who became ill. They uncovered the following information:

- The patients ranged in age from 2 to 73.
- An equal number of males and females were affected. (Ordinarily, females develop hormonal diseases four times more often than males.)
- In most instances, all or nearly all members of a household were affected.
- Friends and coworkers of the sick people did not develop the illness.
- In one family, a mother and son who did not live in the same household both became ill.
- About half the patients lived on farms. Only two cases were found in the largest city in the area.

Solving the Problem

QUESTIONS
1. Based on what you know about the disease at this point, develop a hypothesis about its cause.
2. One person wondered, "Can you catch the disease from a person who has it?" What would you tell this person? Explain your reasoning.

Some people suggested that something in the environment might have caused the outbreak. If so, then why did it affect some people and not others? The doctors worked to identify some experience that was common to the sick people but not to the well people. They decided to conduct a study of 50 of the ill people. They also studied 50 well people who were similar in age, sex, and place of residence.

QUESTIONS
3. Why is it necessary to include well people in the study?
4. What types of questions would you ask the participants in the study? Remember that the goal is to pinpoint differences in the experiences of the two groups.

After completing the study and analyzing the data collected, the doctors discovered that the sick people had one thing in common n they all had eaten lean ground beef from the same meat-packing house. None of the well people had eaten the meat. Although the doctors had pinpointed the source of the problem, one puzzling question remained. How could the beef have caused the high thyroxine levels?

QUESTIONS
5. Propose a hypothesis to explain how the beef might have caused this disease.
6. How could you test your hypothesis? What observations or experiments would you perform? What would the results indicate?
7. Suppose you were one of the doctors who unravelled the mystery of the thyroid disease outbreak. What additional questions might you still have about the disease?

Student Activity 4.2 A Medical Intern Assignment

Teacher Background

<u>Expected Answers</u>

ANALYSIS PART A

1. Organ: pancreas, both endocrine and exocrine function impaired.
2. Cause of the problem is probably alcohol abuse.
3. Fat metabolism is impaired since the pancreas is not producing the enzyme lipase. This is indicated by the low level of serum lipase shown in the lab results.
4. If the function of the pancreas is impaired, the secretion of insulin is probably also low. This can be detected by the very high levels of blood glucose. In the absence of the hormone insulin, glucose does not leave the blood nor enter the cells.
5. Abdominal pain: destruction and inflammation of pancreas
   Weight loss: malabsorption of fat, inefficient use of glucose
   Loss of energy: inefficient use of glucose
   Increased urination: decreased water reabsorption in kidney due to high amounts of glucose causing a change in the osmotic pressure
   Increased thirst: homeostatic mechanism to replace excess fluid loss in urination

ANALYSIS PART B

1. a. After the initial rise in glucose, the levels fall. The change occurs due to the release of insulin which stimulates increased glucose uptake by the cells.
   b. In the normal patient, the level of blood glucose is brought down quite quickly by insulin action. Patient MK's blood glucose decreases at a much slower rate. Therefore, this patient must not be releasing as much insulin as a healthy patient.
2. a. Both graphs exhibit a flat portion or plateau, although Patient MK's is much shorter. At this point the blood glucose has been brought down to normal and insulin release is suppressed.

   b. Even though Patient MK's body has been able to bring the blood glucose down, it is still being maintained at a relatively high level.
3. Point D reflects an increase in blood glucose. The body must need more glucose so glucagon is released to promote glucose production from glycogen. The body could also meet the demand for glucose by eating, which is not the case here.
4. Insulin is released in response to the high levels of blood glucose. At this point glucagon is suppressed. When glucose levels became too low to fulfil the body's needs, glucagon is released and insulin release is suppressed.
5. a. Patient MK has diabetes mellitus.
   b. Start on insulin therapy (injections), and modify diet.
6. a. Problems with digestion and absorption of fat and protein.
   b. Diet modifications with lowered levels of fat and protein, injections of pancreatic lipase and amylase.

Student Activity 4.2 A Medical Intern Assignment

Just the Facts

You are a medical intern in a large city hospital. Part of your evaluation depends on your ability to analyze and diagnose certain medical problems. On your rounds today, the resident introduces you to your next case.

Patient MK has been admitted with severe abdominal pain and frequent vomiting. Other presenting symptoms include weight loss, loss of energy, increased thirst, and frequent urination. The patient's records reveal a history of alcoholism.

A battery of tests have been completed with the following results:

Blood Tests	Normal Values	Patient
serum amylase	50-200 u/dL	15 u/dL
serum lipase	0-1.5 u/mL	0.2 /mL
blood glucose	60-100 mg/dL	139 mg/dL

Urinalysis		
amylase	80-5000 u/24 h	40 u/24 h
glucose	250 mg/24 h	500mg/24 h
ketone bodies	negative	40 mg/24 h

Fecal Fat Levels		
	6 g/day	15 g/day

Analysis Part A

1. What organ or system is implicated in the patient's problems, based on the presenting symptoms and lab test results? Why?
2. After reviewing Patient MK's records and lab tests, what do you think has caused the problem?
3. The amount of fat remaining in the fecal material is much higher than normal. This occurrence is called steatorrhoea. Normally the body metabolizes fat in the digestive process. Why is this not occurring for Patient MK?
4. Urinalysis indicates that the levels of glucose in Patient MK's urine are elevated. Why is this important product of digestion not being used?
5. Choose any two symptoms and explain why Patient MK is experiencing them. Your initial diagnosis lead you to believe that your patient is experiencing chronic pancreatitis. This condition is seen most frequently in patients who have a history of alcoholism. The destruction of the cells of the pancreas is the end result.

Analysis Part B

You order a glucose tolerance test to help verify one part of your diagnosis. In this test, Patient MK receives a specified glucose load, given in the form of a sweetened drink. The patient's blood glucose levels are monitored for the next 3X4 h to determine the body's ability to remove glucose from the bloodstream.

The following graph represents your patient's glucose tolerance curve. A normal curve has also been provided for comparison.

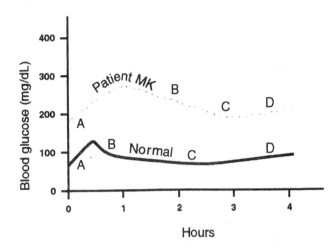

1. a. Initially, the blood glucose is expected to rise in both the patients and the normal control (Point A). What happens after the initial rise in glucose levels? Why does this change occur?
   b. Compare the shape of both the graphs at point B. Explain the reason for the difference seen between the patient and the control.

2. a. Compare the shape of both graphs at point C. What is occurring in the patient's and the control's bodies at this point?
   b. What is one significant difference between the two curves at Point C?

3. Monitoring of blood glucose was continued and point D reflects Patient MK's blood glucose several hours after administering the test. Why is this change in blood glucose occurring?

4. Two hormones are responsible for blood glucose control. Indicate at which points on the graph these two hormones are released or suppressed.

5. a. From your analysis of the glucose tolerance test, what can you conclude about Patient MK?

   b. What would you do to control this problem?

6. a. Originally Patient MK was also diagnosed with reduced output of pancreatic enzymes. What problems will this cause?

   b. What would you do to alleviate this problem?

Student Activity 4.3 Homeostasis Case Study

Teacher Background

Guideline Objective

To begin a homeostasis unit, one teaching suggestion is to review the effects of temperature, pH, ion concentration, and toxic substances on enzyme activity and cell physiology. The use of case studies maximizes student interest in this unit of study and encourages students to hone their critical-thinking skills.

Notes about curare

Curare is a drug used by South American native people to make poisoned darts and arrows. The drug, extracted from the bark of some South American plants, acts to bind with neuron receptors and prevents them carrying out their normal activities. As a result, skeletal muscles subjected to curare, cannot contract, even in the presence of significant quantities of acetylcholine.

This neural impulse blockage, in turn, results in a relaxed muscle paralysis, potentially leading to the cessation of breathing, suffocation, and death of the organism.

Curare is, however, used medically, in a controlled manner, to treat severe muscle spasms which might interfere with a surgical procedure. In addition to its presence in plants, it has also been suggested that curare is found in some of the poisonous frogs of Central and South America.

Evaluation Ideas

For Day 1, consider	Question 1	3 marks
	Question 2	3 marks
	Question 3	4 marks
For Days 2-6, written Report		15 marks
	Total	25 marks

Notes

_____

_____

_____

_____

_____

_____

_____

_____

_____

_____

_____

_____

_____

_____

_____

_____

_____

_____

Student Activity 4.3 Homeostasis Case Study

Day 1

Read the case study. You will have 20 min to complete the following:

1. Identify three specific pieces of information given that are relevant to this unit of study.
2. List three additional pieces of information that would help you to answer/solve this problem (i.e., make up three questions that need to be answered).
3. Which of the pieces of information or the questions you asked in question 2 do you think will be most important when you solve this problem? Justify your choice from a physiological viewpoint.

Make a copy of your answers to the above questions. Keep one and submit the other to be marked. Note that there may be more than one correct answer for each step.

Case Study

Michelle was an archaeology major. As part of their final undergraduate year, all students in this course of study had to participate in a dig. Michelle chose to go to South America to an ancient Inca city that she had read about. The site was located high in the mountains. During the second month at the site, Michelle unearthed an old Indian arrowhead. She had seen several before but none in such good condition.

In spite of her careful handling, Michelle grazed her finger with the surprisingly sharp piece. Thinking nothing of it, she continued with her work; after all she had cut herself before. Within a short time she began to drop things and had difficulty maintaining her balance when she stood up. She went to the site doctor and reported her symptoms, which now included chest pains, stomach cramps, and difficulty breathing. Michelle was immediately transferred to the nearest hospital. Later she found out that several of the arrowheads at the site contained traces of curare.

What happened to Michelle?

Day 2-6

Research the situation illustrated in this case study, paying particular attention to the concept of homeostasis. In one week, hand in a written report based on the answer to question 3. This report is NOT to exceed 250 words!

Student Activity 4.4 A Medical Detective Activity

Teacher Background

This exercise is designed for a Homeostasis unit in biology. Using normal blood test values, patients' blood test values, and patients' symptoms, students will diagnose the diseases. You could extend the activity by asking the students to demonstrate the hormonal control involved in each case. This activity could be done individually or in small groups.

You may wish to photocopy the table of normal blood test results for the student groups.

Case #1
ADDITIONAL CLUES: diminished bmr, thick skin, and coarse hair.
ANSWER: Ms Havers has myxoedema. She is suffering from hypothyroidism. Patients are sluggish, have coarse voices, hair, and skin. They have reduced BMR and poor tolerance to cold. Treatment involves hormone supplements to compensate.

Case #2
ADDITION CLUES: bow-legged, low socioeconomic family situation.
ANSWER: Jason has rickets caused by vitamin D deficiency. He is also exhibiting hypocalcemia (low calcium levels). Treatment involves immediate infusion of calcium into the plasma to stop the spasms. Also, the patient should be studied further to determine if the parathyroid is damaged or has a tumor affecting the output of PTH.

Case #3
ADDITIONAL CLUES: Giuseppe also says he has excessive thirst.
ANSWER: Mr. Agnoli has diabetes, mature onset. This could be caused by overweight or there may be a familial link. He should be stabilized with insulin and undergo education on diet and treatment of diabetes.

Case #4
ADDITIONAL CLUES: Mr. King received several kidney punches during the fight. He was hemorrhaging when he arrived at the hospital.
ANSWER: Mr. King may still be hemorrhaging and may need surgery to correct the problem. Alternatively the kidney punches could have severely damaged his adrenal cortex. This would lead to reduced production of aldosterone. He will need hormone replacement and dietary adjustments to compensate.

Case #5
ADDITIONAL CLUES: Jana has protruding eyeballs. She appears to have a growth or swelling in the front of her neck. She has a high BMR, and she is irritable.
ANSWER: Jana has hyperthyroidism. It could be the result of an autoimmune disease (Grave's disease), which causes stimulation of hormone production, or a tumor in the thyroid. Treatment could include surgery to remove a portion of the thyroid and thus reduce the level of hormones. Alternatively, treatment could involve hormone therapy.

Normal Blood Test Results

TEST	RESULT
Glucose	3.9 - 5.9 mmol/L
Sodium	135 - 145 mol/L
Potassium	3.5 - 5.5 mmol/L
Calcium	2.15 - 2.65 mol/L
Iron	5 - 33 mmol/L
T3	0.24 - 0.36 mol/L
T4	62 - 160 mmol/L

References: Kapit, W. et al. *The Physiology Colouring Book*. Harper Collins, 1987.
Normal lab results are from a clinical laboratory.

Student Activity 4.4 A Medical Detective Activity

You and your partner(s) are interns in a major hospital. In your first assignment, you are working in Internal Medicine. For rounds tomorrow morning, you will be responsible for presenting the cases listed below to the Chief Resident and other attending doctors. There are five patients to be presented. You are responsible for the following for each patient:

a. Summarize the relevant symptoms.
b. Make a diagnosis.
c. Describe the disease effects.
d. Recommend treatment or referral.

Case #1

Mary Havers is a 56-year-old female. She came to the hospital complaining of tiredness and feeling cold. She has a husky voice and a puffy face. She is 10 kg overweight. Her sinuses and throat are clear. There is no evidence of infection as throat swabs are negative and eosinophils are normal. A series of blood tests were done and the results are shown below.

TEST	RESULT	NOTES
Glucose	4.2 mmol/L	
Sodium	138 mmol/L	
Potassium	4.0 mmol/L	
Calcium	2.3 mmol/L	
Iron	21 mmol/L	
T3	0.16 mmol/L	
T4	40 mmol/L	

Case #2

Jason Brown is a young boy, aged four. His mother brought him to the hospital emergency department because he was suffering from spastic contractions of his muscles, including spasms in his respiratory muscles. After he was admitted to hospital, an airway was inserted and a respirator attached. He appeared to be extremely underweight for his age. A series of blood tests were done and the results are shown below.

TEST	RESULT	NOTES
Glucose	3.9 mmol/L	
Sodium	140 mmol/L	
Potassium	4.0 mmol/L	
Calcium	1.85 mmol/L	
Iron	6 mmol/L	
T3	0.30 mmol/L	
T4	85 mmol/L	

Case #3

Giuseppe Agnoli, age 46, was brought by his wife to the hospital. He complained of frequent urination and tiredness. He was tested for urinary infection but results were negative. He was 7 kg overweight for his age. He showed evidence of dehydration in his skin and was disoriented. He was given a saline solution to hydrate him. A series of blood tests were done with the following results.

TEST	RESULT	NOTES
Glucose	12.3 mmol/L	
Sodium	135 mmol/L	
Potassium	3.8 mmol/L	
Calcium	2.45 mmol/L	
Iron	28 mmol/L	
T3	0.35 mmol/L	
T4	128 mmol/L	

Case #4

Jerome King is an 18-year-old man, training to become a professional boxer. He was in a scheduled fight the day before he entered the hospital. It was a difficult fight but he was declared the winner. That night, he collapsed, and his trainer brought him to the hospital. He has low blood pressure, and has an appropriate weight for his build. He has been passing blood in his urine and stool (feces). He was given a number of blood tests with the following results. Immediately after the tests he was given two units of blood and underwent surgery. However, he has not shown any improvement, i.e., his blood results have stayed the same.

TEST	RESULT	NOTES
Glucose	5.6 mmol/L	
Sodium	115 mmol/L	
Potassium	6.0 mmol/L	
Calcium	2.50 mmol/L	
Iron	22 mmol/L	
T3	0.30 mmol/L	
T4	110 mmol/L	

Case #5

Jana Chapeau is 23 years old. She is 10 kg underweight for her frame. She is nervous and fidgets during examination. Jana complains that she notices her heart racing and she is extremely tired. She says that she eats well despite her thinness and is sensitive to the heat. A series of blood tests gave the following results.

TEST	RESULT	NOTES
Glucose	4.8 mmol/L	
Sodium	138 mmol/L	
Potassium	4.4 mmol/L	
Calcium	2.3 mmol/L	
Iron	24 mmol/L	
T3	0.45 mmol/L	
T4	190 mmol/L	

Student Activity 4.5 A Nephron Activity

Teacher Background

Before starting this activity, students should review osmosis, active transport, filtration, and reabsorption. See the questions at the beginning of the student pages.

Activity: Think/Pair/Share

1. Give each student a copy of the attached handout. Explain that samples of nephron contents were removed at different locations along the nephron. The locations were tested for flow rate, and the samples were analyzed for the concentrations of protein, glucose, urea, sodium ions, and ammonium ions. The flow rate index is given in numbers that are relative to each other (i.e., a rate of "100" is relatively fast moving and a rate of "1" is relatively slow moving). The concentrations are also given in relative terms (i.e., a concentration of "6a" would be 6 times as concentrated as a concentration of "a").

2. Have the students read through the information individually, checking to see how rates and concentrations change with each location.

3. Ask the students to answer the questions on the student pages with a partner. Have them share their ideas and answer the questions to the best of their abilities.

4. Discuss answers with the entire class, using ideas from all pairs. As you do this, create a report together, using the headings from the following tabular format.

Expected Answers

The Formation of Urine in the Nephron

Site in nephron	What is occurring?	Mechanisms involved
Glomerulus/Bowman's Capsule	Water, glucose, amino acids, salts, and nitrogenous wastes (smaller molecules) move through capillary walls of the glomerulus into the Bowman's capsule. (The useful molecules and ions need to be recovered later.)	Filtration: high blood pressure forces smaller molecules into the Bowman's capsule.
1st Convolution (proximal convoluted tubule)	Reabsorption of useful molecules (glucose, amino acids)	Active Transport: molecules are forced back into the bloodstream against a concentration gradient.
Loop of Henle	Salts move into surrounding tissue Water is reabsorbed into the bloodstream, therefore conc. of sodium and ammonium ions and urea molecules increases	Diffusion Osmosis (surrounding tissues are hypertonic to liquid in tubules))
2nd Convolution (distal convoluted tubule)	Reabsorption of useful molecules (glucose, amino acids)	Active Transport
Urine Collecting Duct (collecting tubule)	More water passes outward. Concentrated filtrate flows down the collecting duct into the bladder for eventual elimination.	Osmosis Pressure flow

Student Activity 4.5 A Nephron Activity

Key Question

How is urine produced in the nephron? Before you start this activity, review the following:
1. Define osmosis, active transport, filtration, reabsorption
2. Where is the kidney located in the body? Where is it relative to other organs that are involved in the digestive and circulatory systems?
3. What is a nephron? How does its function relate to the kidney as a whole?
4. What are the parts of the nephron?

Activity: Think/Pair/Share

1. Read this handout carefully. Samples of nephron contents were removed at different locations along the nephron. The locations were tested for flow rate and the samples were analyzed for concentrations of protein, glucose, urea, sodium ions, and ammonium ions. The flow rate index is given in numbers that are relative to each other (i.e., a rate of "100" is relatively fast moving and a rate of "1" is relatively slow moving). The concentrations are also given in relative terms (i.e., a concentration of "6a" would be 6 times as concentrated as a concentration of "a").
2. Read through the information individually, checking to see how rates and concentrations differ for each sample.
3. Answer the following questions by yourself. Then, with a partner, share your ideas, answering the questions to the best of your abilities.
   a. How does the initial blood plasma differ from the final urine sample?
   b. Copy the following chart and fill it in. You may guess if you don't know the answer.

Sample #	Position in nephron	How is this sample different from the previous samples?	What might have caused these changes? (mechanisms)
blood plasma			
1			
2			
3			

4. The answers will be discussed with the entire class, using ideas from all pairs. The following format will be used to create a summary of all of the class findings.

The Formation of Urine in the Nephron

Site in nephron	What is occurring?	Mechanisms involved
Glomerulus/Bowman's Capsule		
proximal convoluted tubule		
Loop of Henle		
distal convoluted tubule		
collecting tubule		

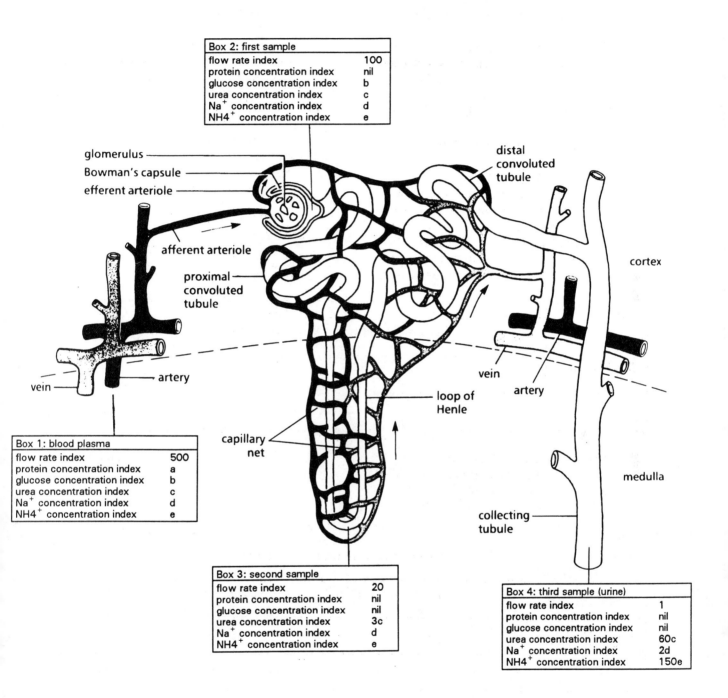

Box 2: first sample

flow rate index	100
protein concentration index	nil
glucose concentration index	b
urea concentration index	c
Na$^+$ concentration index	d
NH4$^+$ concentration index	e

glomerulus

Bowman's capsule

efferent arteriole

distal convoluted tubule

afferent arteriole

proximal convoluted tubule

cortex

vein — artery

artery

vein

loop of Henle

capillary net

medulla

collecting tubule

Box 1: blood plasma

flow rate index	500
protein concentration index	a
glucose concentration index	b
urea concentration index	c
Na$^+$ concentration index	d
NH4$^+$ concentration index	e

Box 3: second sample

flow rate index	20
protein concentration index	nil
glucose concentration index	nil
urea concentration index	3c
Na$^+$ concentration index	d
NH4$^+$ concentration index	e

Box 4: third sample (urine)

flow rate index	1
protein concentration index	nil
glucose concentration index	nil
urea concentration index	60c
Na$^+$ concentration index	2d
NH4$^+$ concentration index	150e

Section 5
Genetics

Student Activity 5.1 Human Pedigree Analysis

When you hear the word "pedigree" you usually think of dogs or cattle, referring to the purity of breed of the animal's ancestors. However, pedigrees can be drawn to follow the genetic history of any species, including human families and related individuals. Pedigree charts are diagrams which use circles, squares and connecting lines to show the family "tree." They can also be used to show the inheritance of a particular trait through several generations. Pedigree charts are often constructed if a couple who plans to have children is at risk of passing on harmful conditions or diseases.

Project

1. For this project, refer to a textbook or reference having information on human pedigrees.
2. From the list of inherited human traits given in the table below, construct one or two pedigrees depending on the number of complete generations of your family that you can include.
   a. If you have access to at least three generations, choose one trait and construct a pedigree to show the pattern of its inheritance in your family.
   b. If you have access to fewer than three generations, choose two traits and produce a family pedigree for each.

Note: You must choose a trait where both dominant and recessive phenotypes can be demonstrated.

Questions

1. a. Predict the genotypes of each member of your pedigree. (Draw a table using a number for each individual including spouses.)
   b. On your table, indicate the individuals for whom you can make a definite genotype identification.
2. With reference to your answer to 1b, explain:
   a. why you can be certain of one person's genotype.
   b. why you cannot be certain of another person's genotype.
3. Predict the genotypes and phenotypes, for one trait only, of all possible offspring if you were mated with a heterozygote for that trait.

List of Inherited Human Traits

	Dominant	Recessive
Ear Lobes	free	attached
Hairline	widow's peak	no widow's peak
Tongue Rolling	roller	non-roller
Hand Clasping	left thumb on top	right thumb on top
Finger Mid-Joint Hair	present	absent
Thumb (See Figure)	straight	hitch-hiker's thumb
Chin Cleft	present	absent

Student Activity 5.1 (continued)

In this figure, the upper hand exhibits the "hitch-hiker's thumb" trait.

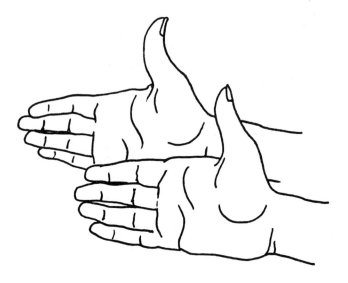

Student Activity 5.2 A Chromosome Mapping Activity

Teacher Background

The following chromosome mapping assignment is for a Senior Biology genetics unit. The data are from the Sourcebook for the Biological Sciences, 3rd ed., 1986, page 532.

Chromosome Map Answer is not drawn to scale.

Marking Scheme for Chromosome Mapping

1. Proper completion of the chart	· 0	1	2	
2. Scaled chromosome map				
- correct scale	0	1	2	
- correct sequence of loci	0	1	2	
- correct spacing of loci	0	1	2	
- position of centromere	0	1	2	
3. Question 2	0	1	2	
4. Question 3	0	1	2	3
Total	/15			

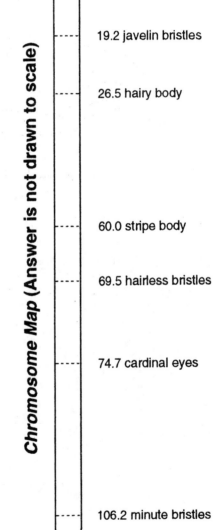

0.1 veinlet veins

19.2 javelin bristles

26.5 hairy body

60.0 stripe body

69.5 hairless bristles

74.7 cardinal eyes

106.2 minute bristles

Chromosome Map (Answer is not drawn to scale)

Student Activity 5.2 A Chromosome Mapping Activity

The following data were collected from repeated breedings of fruit flies (*D. melanogaster*). The data record the frequency, to 0.1 percent, of the recombinant characteristics for seven genes located on the same side of the centromere on chromosome 3.

The veinlet vein gene is located 0.1 mapping units from the centromere and acts as an effective base point for comparison.

1. Prepare a scaled Chromosome Map for Drosophila chromosome 3, using a scale of 1 mapping unit = 3.0 mm. Show the locations of the seven genes plus the veinlet veins gene.

2. Explain your reasoning for the location of the following loci:
   a. hairy body
   b. hairless bristles
   c. scarlet eyes

3. State three reasons why the chromosomes of Drosophila melanogaster are more completely mapped than those of Homo sapiens.

	Scarlet eyes	Cardinal eyes	Javelin bristles	Stripe body	Minute bristles	Hairy body	Hairless bristles
Scarlet eyes	---		24.8	18.0			
Cardinal eyes		---		12.7	31.5		
Javelin Bristles			---			7.3	50.3
Stripe body				---		35.5	
Minute bristles					---		36.7
Veinlet veins		74.6				26.4	
Hairy body						---	43.0

Student Activity 5.3 **Human Genetic Traits**

Teacher Background

Purpose

Using prepared cards showing genetic traits, along with traits determined by the students, this activity will help the students understand genes and traits (also known as phenotypes); that genes coding for traits usually occur in two forms, a dominant and a recessive; and whether the sex of the individual is a factor.

Background Information

Define gene and trait.

Preparation

Prepare enough cards for the entire class, taking into account the number of boys and girls. Each card should look something like the one on this page.

Leave space for the student's name, but fill in sex, blood type, color blindness, and eye color. The remaining traits will be filled in by the individual student. As the teacher, you control three of the traits (as well as the class ratios for those three traits if so desired), and the rest of the traits are determined by the class itself.

Sample Card Set

To ensure the success of this activity, prepare the cards with appropriate proportions based on each trait. If the class size is 26, prepare 26 cards with the following traits:

Blood type: O: 12; A: 6; B: 5; AB: 3
Eye color: brown: 18; blue: 8
Color blindness: normal vision: 21; red-green
                  color blind: 5

Since blood type and eye color do not depend on the sex of the individual, there can be relatively equal numbers of boys and girls in each of the blood types or eye colors. For example, of the 12 people in the class with type O blood, 7 could be girls and 5 could be boys.

Because red-green color blindness is a sex-linked trait, the numbers should reflect the fact that more boys are color blind than girls. For example, if the class includes 14 girls and 12 boys, of the 21 people with normal vision, 14 of them would be female (i.e., all the females have normal vision) and 7 would be male. The 5 who are color blind are all male.

Procedure

1. Provide the prepared cards in two piles, one for girls and one for boys.
2. Each student picks a card.
3. Have the students in pairs fill in the missing genetic traits on their card based on their own phenotypes.
4. Appoint a student as the class recorder and fill in the following table on the board.

NAME:	*John*
SEX:	*male*
Genetic Traits	
Blood type:	*O*
Color Blindness:	*normal vision*
Eye Color:	*brown*
Ear lobes:	*(detached/attached)*
Hitch-hiker's thumb:	*(hitch-hiker's thumb/straight thumb)*
Tongue rolling:	*(roll/can't roll)*
Right or left handed:	*(right/left)*
Hair Color:	*(dark/light)*

A page of model cards are provided in Appendix B.

		Student				
		1	2...	...	...26	Total
Sex	male					
	female					
Blood type	O					
	A					
	B					
	AB					
Color blindness	normal					
	color blind					
	brown					
	blue					
Hitch-hiker's thumb	yes					
	no					
Ear lobe	detached					
	attached					
Tongue rolling	roller					
	non-roller					
Right/left handed	right					
	left					
Hair color	dark					
	light					

Teacher Reference

	Dominant	Recessive
Color blindness	normal vision	color blind
Eye color	brown	blue
Ear lobes	detached	attached
Hitch-hiker's thumb	hitch-hiker's	straight thumb
Tongue rolling	tongue roller	non-tongue roller
Right/left handed	right handed	left handed
Hair color	dark	light

Note: Blood type is not an example of alleles existing in only two forms. Type A and type B are dominant over type O, and type AB is an example of co-dominance. See the explanation in the activity "Mystery at the Termond Estate."

Student Activity 5.3 Human Genetic Traits

Answer the following questions.

1. Based on your results, which traits do you think are dominant and which are recessive?
2. Compare the class results to the teacher's list that indicates which form of each trait is dominant or recessive. Were any traits listed as dominant rare in your class? Were any traits listed as recessive common? Why might this happen? Explain.
3. What do you think dominant and recessive mean?
4. In this discovery lab, most of the traits that we looked at seemed to come in only two forms. What was the one exception to this general rule?

Research: This exception is an example of multiple alleles. Write a summary that clearly defines the following terms: allele, gene, genotype, phenotype, dominant, and recessive. Explain the multiple allele system.

5. Look over the class results and decide if the sex of the individual is significant in any particular trait.

Research: Traits that depend on the sex of the individual are called sex-linked traits. Write a one-page summary that clearly explains the concept of sex-linked traits and give at least two more examples of sex-linked traits that occur in humans.

Teaching Notes

_____

_____

_____

_____

_____

_____

_____

_____

_____

_____

_____

_____

_____

_____

_____

_____

_____

_____

Student Activity 5.4 **Mystery at the Termond Estate**

Teacher Background

"Mystery at the Termond Estate" is a logical problem-solving activity intended for use in a second-year or advanced placement biology course containing a unit on Genetic Continuity. It involves an introduction to Mendelian genetics and some of the variations of Mendel's Principles. It is probably best used after the following topics are introduced:

1. the concept of monohybrid crosses
2. the ABO blood types and genetics of co-dominance
3. the Rh factor and its genetics
4. pedigree symbols and construction, and the use of pedigree diagrams in genetic problem solving

Students need to understand that the ear-lobe shape, ABO blood type and Rh factor are determined by the alleles of single genes. Attached ear lobes (recessive) connect directly to the head, while free ear lobes (dominant) hang down. Rh-positive individuals (dominant) have the Rh protein present on the surface of their erythrocytes (red blood cells), while Rh-negative individuals (recessive) lack this particular surface protein on their erythrocytes.

There are three possible alleles which determine the ABO blood type: I^A, I^B, and i. Any two of these alleles in combination determine an individual's ABO blood type. Both I^A and I^B are codominant alleles, which produce erythrocyte surface proteins A and B. The i allele is recessive and does not cause the production of either A or B proteins. Thus, a person with the genotype ii has type O blood, a person with genotype I^Ai or I^AI^A has type A blood, a person with genotype I^Bi or I^BI^B has type B blood, and a person with genotype I^AI^B has type AB blood.

In this problem, students must integrate their knowledge of single gene inheritance as outlined above together with an understanding of pedigree analysis and logical thinking.

Solution

Since the blood type on the safe was ARh-, the only possible suspects are Janette, Ellen, Olivia and Lorne. However, the thief also had attached ear lobes. This leaves only Ellen and Olivia as possible suspects with An blood and attached ear lobes. In order to determine which one of these women is the thief, the individual who is not a blood relative must first be identified.

Students will need to look carefully at the blood types, Rh factors, and ear shapes of the offspring and compare these directly with their parents to determine whether these types are possible. All of the ABO and ear-lobe characteristics of the children and grandchildren are possible from their respective parents (Count Ralph must have been type A or B) except Alan. Alan is Rh positive while both his parents are negative. This is not normally possible, suggesting that he was adopted or fathered by someone other than Richard who is a true son of Ralph and Marie. It can be concluded that Olivia (type An with attached ear lobes) is the thief because she wanted a share of her father-in-law's estate for her son Alan who is not a blood relative of Count Ralph. Ellen also has Rh negative blood and attached ears, but her parents, though both Rh positive, could have been heterozygous, thus allowing Ellen to be Rh negative. She also has no motive for the theft.

Note: Students should have little difficulty in narrowing down the suspects to Ellen and Olivia. They will probably have more difficulty identifying the non-blood relative. They may benefit from some coaching after they have struggled on their own for a while.

Teaching Strategies

This activity could be used in several ways:
1. As an individual assignment to reinforce the ABO and Rh blood types, pedigrees, and monohybrid crosses.
2. As a small group assignment where 2 or 3 students put their heads together to solve the problem.
3. As a unique method of evaluating the content in 1. above, together with testing problem solving.

Solution: Mystery at Termond Estate

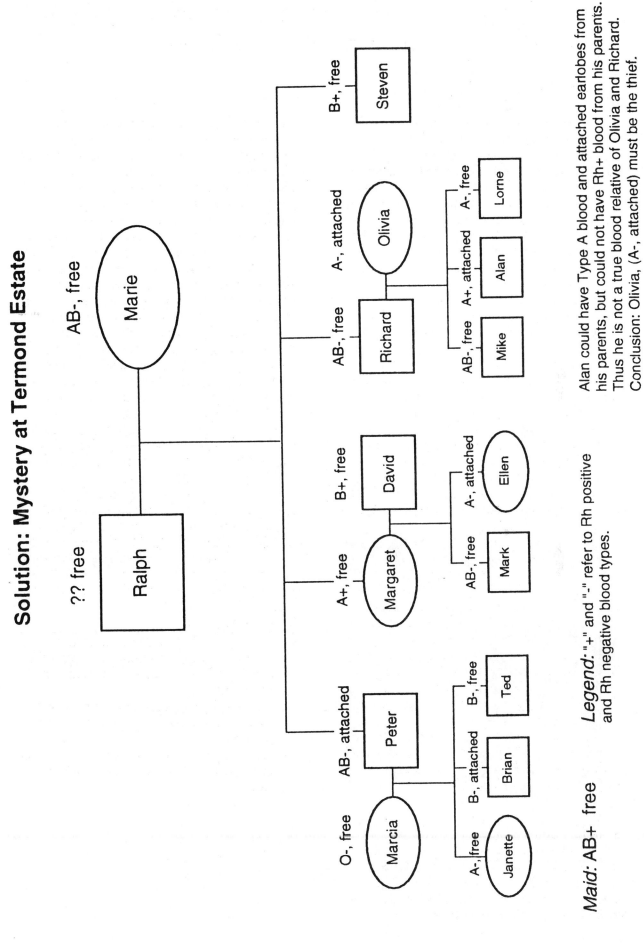

Ralph
?? free

Marie
AB-, free

Peter
AB-, attached

Marcia
O-, free

Margaret
A+, free

David
B+, free

Richard
AB-, free

Olivia
A-, attached

Steven
B+, free

Janette
A-, free

Brian
B-, attached

Ted
B-, free

Mark
AB-, free

Ellen
A-, attached

Mike
AB-, free

Alan
A+, attached

Lorne
A-, free

Alan could have Type A blood and attached earlobes from his parents, but could not have Rh+ blood from his parents. Thus he is not a true blood relative of Olivia and Richard. Conclusion: Olivia, (A-, attached) must be the thief.

Legend: "+" and "-" refer to Rh positive and Rh negative blood types.

Maid: AB+ free

Student Activity 5.4 Mystery at the Termond Estate

Count Ralph and his wife Marie, owners of the Termond Estate, were an elderly couple of some wealth. Ralph died suddenly when he was struck by lightning in his metal rowboat while fishing in Termond Lake. His body was never recovered. All Count Ralph's children and grandchildren (who happened to be at the estate at the time for a Father's Day celebration), eagerly awaited the reading of Count Ralph's will, since they all knew that the will would provide each blood relative with an equal share of his estate wealth.

When the lawyer arrived, he noticed that a sum of money had been stolen from Count Ralph's safe. The sum missing was equal to one person's portion of the estate value. In addition, a small amount of fresh blood was found on the inside of the safe door, presumably belonging to the thief. As this news was being announced by the lawyer, the maid rushed into the room and revealed that she had walked into Count Ralph's study and observed the thief quickly slipping out of the patio doors. She had not seen the face or been able to identify the thief, since he or she wore a mask and a bulky overcoat. She did see, however, that the thief had an attached ear lobe.

Police Detective Morse was called to the Termond Estate. Upon his arrival, he immediately ordered blood typing tests on all in the house, and on the blood smeared on the safe (found to be Type An). He also noted the ear-lobe type of everyone. After perusing the data, Morse called all of the relatives together and announced that he had discovered the identity of the thief. One of the children or grandchildren was not really a blood relative, and the theft of the money was to ensure a share in the inheritance.

Use Morse's data table below and your knowledge of ABO and Rh blood typing as well as your knowledge of inheritance of ear-lobe shape to solve this mystery. Construct a pedigree using the data table, and use it to organize the data.

Questions

1. Who was the thief? Explain how Morse was able to identify the thief.
2. For which individual was the money intended? (Who was not the true blood relative?)

Morse's Data Table			
Name	Blood type	Ear Shape	Parents/Relationship
Ralph	?	free	N/A
Marie	ABn	free	N/A
Marcia	On	free	married to Peter
Peter	ABn	attached	Ralph & Marie
Margaret	A+	free	Ralph & Marie
David	B+	free	married to Margaret
Richard	ABn	free	Ralph & Marie
Olivia	An	attached	married to Richard
Steven	B+	free	Ralph & Marie
Janette	An	free	Marcia & Peter
Brian	Bn	attached	Marcia & Peter
Ted	Bn	free	Marcia & Peter
Mark	ABn	free	Margaret & David
Ellen	An	attached	Margaret & David
Mike	ABn	free	Richard & Olivia
Alan	A+	attached	Richard & Olivia
Lorne	An	free	Richard & Olivia
maid	AB+	free	N/A

Section 6
Evolution

Student Activity 6.1 Evolution and Proteins

Introduction

The letters in the following chart represent amino acids found in the cytochrome-c protein complex of a number of different organisms. Changes in amino acid sequence occur as a result of mutations in the DNA that codes for that protein. Therefore, the more amino acids that two organisms have in common, the more closely related they are in terms of evolution. In other words, there has been less time for mutations to occur between the present organisms and their common ancestors.

Compare the amino acid sequences of the cytochrome-c proteins of the organisms listed (only a short portion of the molecule is given). For each pair of organisms, find the number of identical amino acids and write that number on the table.

Human:	ASDFGHJKLQ
Monkey:	ASDFTHJKLQ
Pig:	AWDFTHJKLQ
Rabbit:	AWDFTHUKLQ
Horse:	AWDFTHUKLP
Dog:	AWDFUHUKLP
Kangaroo:	AWDMUHUKLP

Questions

1. This type of diagram is used to show the evolutionary relationships among species. Species that are closely related are put close together on the diagram, more distantly related species are placed farther apart. Using the number of identical base pairs between the species pairs from the table, complete this diagram.

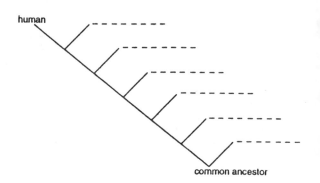

2. This is only one of many ways to determine the evolutionary relationships of species. Discuss other methods of research in this field.

	Human	Monkey	Pig	Rabbit	Horse	Dog	Kangaroo
Human	0						
Monkey	XXX	0					
Pig		XXX	0				
Rabbit	XXX	XXX	XXX	0			
Horse	XXX	XXX	XXX	XXX	0		
Dog	XXX	XXX	XXX	XXX	XXX	0	
Kangaroo	XXX	XXX	XXX	XXX	XXX	XXX	0

Student Activity 6.1 The Dinosaur Extinction: Extraterrestrial Impact or Volcanoes?

Teacher Background

Idea

This assignment consists of having students read several statements from various authors concerning the cause of the dinosaur extinction. Three articles argue extraterrestrial impact, while three argue in support of terrestrial causation (primarily volcanoes). After reading the excerpts from the articles, the students will divide into two teams. Give each team one of the two opinions to defend. An informal debate will follow.

Purpose

The purposes of this activity are:
1. to encourage the students to develop higher order thinking skills;
2. to help the students discover that real science is often filled with debate and controversy, and that by definition, theories can never be proven absolutely true;
3. to develop team-work skills and skills in analyzing, collecting, and presenting data in a persuasive manner; and
4. to learn about a very interesting and controversial part of biological study.

This activity could be included in most units that focus on evolution.

Possible Extensions

When this topic was researched as part of a second-year evolutionary biology course at university level, the author found it to be one of the most interesting areas of biology. Some possible extensions for students could be as follows.
1. Use the articles as the basis for the discussion of evolutionary theories in general.
2. Use the articles as the basis for an Independent Study Unit (I.S.U.) topic for a student or two who are particularly interested.

They should do research, for example, to discover whether any other ideas have emerged since the publication of the articles listed here. If so, do they lend weight to one opinion or the other?

References

Alvarez, L.W., Alvarez, A., Asaro, F., and Michel, H.V. 1980. Extraterrestrial cause for the cretaceous-tertiary extinction. Science 208: 1095.

Hallam, A. 1987. End-cretaceous mass extinction event: argument for terrestrial causation. Science 238: 1237-1241.

Kerr, R.A. 1985. Periodic extinctions and impacts challenged. Science 227: 1451-1453.

Kerr, R.A. 1988. Huge impact is favored k-t boundary killer. Science 242: 865-868.

Moses, C.O. 1989. A geochemical perspective on the causes and periodicity of mass extinctions. Ecology 70: 812-823.

Waldrop. M. M. 1988. After the fall. Science 239: 977-978.

Student Activity 6.2 The Dinosaur Extinction: Extraterrestrial Impact or Volcanoes?

Articles that Support the Meteorite Impact Theory

STATEMENT 1

Platinum metals are depleted in the earth's crust relative to their cosmic abundance; concentrations of these elements in deep-sea sediments may thus indicate influxes of extraterrestrial material. Deep-sea limestones exposed in Italy, Denmark, and New Zealand show iridium increases of about 30, 160, and 20 times, respectively, above the background level at precisely the time of the Cretaceous-Tertiary extinctions, 65 million years ago. Reasons are given to indicate that this iridium is of extraterrestrial origin...

A hypothesis is suggested which accounts for the extinctions and the iridium observations. Impact of a large earth-crossing asteroid would inject about 60 times the object's mass into the atmosphere as pulverized rock; a fraction of this dust would stay in the stratosphere for several years and be distributed worldwide. The resulting darkness would suppress photosynthesis, and the expected biological consequences match quite closely the extinctions observed in the paleontological record...

Four different independent estimates of the diameter of the asteroid give values that are in the range 10 ± 4 km. (Alvarez et al., 1980)

STATEMENT 2

If one assumes that the mass extinctions at the Cretaceous-Tertiary boundary were really caused by the impact of a large comet or asteroid some 65 million years ago, as the evidence increasingly suggests, then conditions at that time were not just bad, they were ghastly. Recent computer models by atmospheric scientists Ronald G. Prinn and Bruce Fegley of the Massachusetts Institute of Technology indicate that the aftermath of such an impact could have included a year of darkness under a smog of nitrogen oxides; waters poisoned by trace metals leached from soil and rock; and global rains as corrosive as battery acid. "The problem isn't to kill species off," said Prinn as he described the findings at the recent AAAS meeting in Boston. "The problem is to think of safe havens where anything could have survived." (Waldrop, 1988)

STATEMENT 3

One advantage held by the theory that a large impact killed off more than 70% of the species living at the end of the age of the dinosaurs is the inevitability of such impacts, given the existence of asteroids and comets that cross Earth's orbit. Globally disastrous eruptions remain hypothetical. Eugene Shoemaker of the U.S. Geological Survey (USGS) in Flagstaff told the conference about his latest estimates of the frequency of large impacts based on discoveries of Earth-crossing asteroids and comets. About every 100 million years on average, Shoemaker concludes, an object 10 km in diameter slams into Earth at perhaps 20 km per second or more, releasing 60 million megatons of energy and creating a 150-km-wide crater. (Kerr, 1988)

Articles that Support the Terrestrial Theory

STATEMENT 4

This hypothesis (referring to the asteroid impact hypothesis) meets with at least four serious objections:

i.   The iridium concentration in comets is probably about an order of magnitude less than the average for iron meteorites, and one would need to invoke successive impacts of perhaps five iron meteorites of the necessary mass over a period of about a million years to account for the successive iridium peaks now recognized at Gubbio; this seems extremely improbable.

ii. It is difficult to see how cometary impact can account for the end of the Cretaceous strontium peak, the kaolinite pulse at Gubbio,

Student Activity 6.2 (continued)

and other evidence of a significant but not geologically instantaneous regression.
iii. The problem of locating plausible impact craters is compounded if there were a succession of impacts.
iv. It has been argued by a group of astronomers that comet showers are not produced with either sufficient frequency or intensity by individual known bodies, whether stars or molecular clouds, to account for either periodic or episodic mass extinctions. (Hallam, 1987)

STATEMENT 5
No one has delivered a knockout punch to the idea put forward more than a year ago that every 28 million years or so a swarm of comets batters Earth and drives as much as 70 percent of animals and plants to extinction. But if it has not been knocked out, the hypothesis is certainly falling back under increasing criticism. Many geologists, paleontologists, astronomers, and statisticians who have now had a chance to study the details of the proposals find the geological evidence merely suggestive or even nonexistent and the supposed underlying mechanisms improbable at best. (Kerr, 1985)

STATEMENT 6
Environmental change, including changes in biogeochemical cycles, climate, and sea level, is the primary cause of extinctions that result from mechanisms external to evolutionary dynamics. Evidence that extraordinary tectonism, including volcanism, sea-floor spreading and eustatic sea level changes, took place prior to and at the Cretaceous-Tertiary boundary (K-TB) is sufficient to account for the environmental changes that led to mass extinctions. A coincident impact of an extraterrestrial object cannot be conclusively ruled out. Some mineralogic evidence suggests a scenario that includes impacts, but this does not rule out tectonism. The K-TB boundary is certainly the best studied and most often discussed extinction boundary, but study of other extinction episodes and other potential extinction causes will now shed more light on mechanisms than continued study of the K-TB. (Moses, 1989)

Notes

_____

_____

_____

_____

_____

_____

_____

_____

_____

_____

_____

Notes (continued)

Section 7
Ecology

What Are the Effects of Human Intervention on a Food Web?

Teacher Background

This activity illustrates one way to show the potential interactions among humans, food webs, and the ecosystem. The example is suitable for use in an introductory unit on ecology.

Some additional information of interest to both teacher and students about the results of spraying DDT on Borneo:

- The geckoes, small lizard-like animals, received nerve damage from eating the cockroaches, and their reflexes were slowed by the DDT;
- Cats were able to catch and prey upon more of the geckoes than before, therefore the cats died from DDT ingestion.
- Because the cats died, rats, having no predators, moved in from the forest. They carried fleas which carried the plague, and humans contracted the plague.
- When geckoes died due to DDT poisoning and being consumed by cats, the caterpillar population increased due to a lack of predators.
- The increase in numbers of caterpillars meant that more of the thatched hut roofs were consumed and the roofs collapsed.

The World Health Organization (WHO) solution was to take more cats to Borneo. These cats also died from eating geckoes slowed by DDT.

Source: Mackean, D.G. 1992. *GSCE Biology*. John Murray Publishers Ltd. London.

Teaching Notes

_____

_____

_____

_____

_____

_____

_____

_____

_____

_____

_____

_____

_____

_____

_____

_____

_____

Student Activity 7.1
What Are the Effects of Human Intervention on a Food Web?

Introduction

In the 1950's, malaria was a severe problem in Borneo. Since malaria is carried and transmitted by mosquitoes, the World Health Organization (WHO) attempted to rid the island of mosquitoes by spraying the populated area with the pesticide DDT.

The diagram below illustrates a food web in the ecosystem. All of the members of the food web were affected by the DDT. Consider the following facts as you study the food web:

1. DDT causes nerve damage, slow reflexes, and eventual (but not usually sudden) death in an animal.
2. When an animal preys upon an animal that has consumed DDT, the predator is affected by the DDT in the prey.
3. Mosquitoes are killed by DDT. Cockroaches are also affected, but not killed, by DDT.

Task

1. Predict the effects of spraying DDT in this ecosystem on each member of the food web.
2. Propose a solution to the problem that resulted from the spraying of DDT.
3. What are some alternative solutions to the malaria problem?

Additional Questions

4. List each member of the food web. Explain the probable effect of DDT on each member. Support your answers with evidence from the diagram and the facts you were given about the effects of DDT on organisms in the food web.
5. Explain why you think your solution (given in question 2 above) will work. Support your ideas with evidence from the diagram and the facts you were given.
6. If a malaria epidemic threatened Borneo in the 1990's, what type of solution could be attempted?

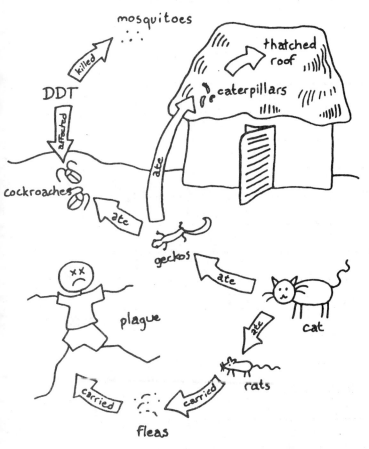

Teacher Activity 7.2 A Food Web Activity

Introduction

This activity is suitable for an introductory Biology unit at grade 9 or 10. Each pair of students receive 12 cards, each with the name of a plant, a herbivore, a carnivore, or a top carnivore. Also, provide the students with 14 arrows. Have available 12 "clue" cards. (Organism and Clue Cards are provided for your use in Appendix B.) Ask students to create a food web using their base knowledge to link the various organisms. If they run into difficulties, they may ask for a "clue" card to help them draw their food web. Deduct marks for each clue card received.

Organism Cards
Fox
Wolf
Berries
Rabbit
Frog
Owl
Snake
Hawk
Mouse
Grain
Grasshopper
Grass

Once they have completed the food web, discuss the following questions in class or ask the students to write the answers.

1. Describe the role of plants in the food web.
2. Identify the herbivores, carnivores, and top carnivores within their food web.
3. Identify the different food chains within the food web.
4. Describe the effects on the food web of:
   - over-population of rabbits.
   - a drought.
   - hunting of wolves by humans.

Clue Cards

1. Snakes are carnivores.
2. A wolf is a top carnivore.
3. Grasshoppers eat grain.
4. Rabbits do not eat grain.
5. Rabbits are herbivores.
6. Frogs eat insects.
7. Hawks eat both herbivores and carnivores.
8. Rodents eat grain.
9. Hawks do not eat rabbits.
10. Snakes eat rodents and amphibians.
11. Owls eat rabbits.
12. Snakes are eaten by birds.

Expected Answer

Some students may require more than 14 arrows. This diagram shows all possible connections within the fod web.

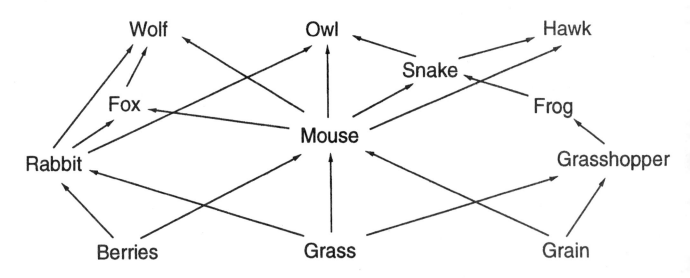

Section 8
A Portfolio Pot-Pourri

Student Activity 8.1 Science Fiction/Fantasy Book Report

Teacher Background

Introduction

The science fiction/fantasy book report (or short story) would be applicable in a Biology or Science course. It links the study of ecology to sensing and responding to the environment. Students are encouraged to explore and analyze alien systems which illustrate physical and behavioral adaptations to a different environment.

This activity integrates science with English and allows those students who have an aptitude for creative writing to express themselves in a manner not commonly encountered in science.

Authors

Piers Anthony	Robert Jordan
Isaac Asimov	Guy Gavriel Kay
Greg Bear	Anne McCaffrey
Terry Brooks	Vonda N. McIntyre
Edgar Rice Burroughs	Larry Niven
	Fredrik Pohl
Arthur C. Clark	Jerry Pournelle
Gordon R. Dickson	Melanie Rawn
David Eddings	Robert Silverberg
Joe Haldeman	J.R.R. Tolkein
Robert A. Heinlein	Tad Williams
	Roger Zelazny

Assessment for Science Fiction/Fantasy Book Report

Criteria and points allotted	Description of criteria parameters	F	D	C	B	A	A+
Title page (10)	The title page includes the title of the novel, the author, the publisher, and the date. The student's name and section as well as the date should be included. The layout and graphics are neat and arranged in a pleasing manner.	3	6	7	8	9	10
Format and grammar (10)	The report contains no spelling errors or major grammatical errors. Proper punctuation is used, paragraphs are indented, and proper pagination and margins are used.	3	6	7	8	9	10
Summary (10)	A clear and concise summary of the main characters, setting, and flow of events is written in an organized and logical manner.	3	6	7	8	9	10
Adaptations (30)	The report includes a description of pertinent environmental (social and economic) factors to which characters have been adapted. Evidence of physical and behavioral adaptation are documented by use of example. Evidence to support relationships between environmental factors and adaptations are presented in a logical and reasoned manner.	10	18	21	24	27	30
Maximum points = 60		/60					

Student Activity 8.1 Science Fiction/Fantasy Book Report

Option 1

1. Read a science fiction or fantasy novel. Your selection must be approved by your teacher. The novel must have an environment different from Earth as we know it today. Books that have been made into movies may not be used.
2. Write a 500-word book report. Summarize the plot briefly. Outline the physical and behavioral adaptations that enable the characters to survive in their particular environment. Relate any unique characteristics of the environment, as well as any relevant social and economic factors, to the adaptations evident in the characters.

Option 2

Write a 2000-word science fiction or fantasy short story which includes character living in a peculiar environment. Describe the parameters of the alien environment, and any physical and behavioral adaptations that enable the characters to survive.

Sources

A selection of books available in your school or public library. (For help, consult the librarians.)

Notes

_____
_____
_____
_____
_____
_____
_____
_____
_____
_____
_____
_____
_____
_____
_____
_____
_____
_____
_____
_____
_____

Teacher Activity 8.2 Graphic Organizers

Introduction

Graphic organizers are diagrammatic representations of relationships among concepts. They provide a meaningful framework specific to a domain of knowledge (Novak, 1990). Visual organizers can be used at all grade levels and can take on several different roles. A very general organizer can be used as an introduction to a topic, or a detailed organizer could help students review a concept, topic, or course.

Graphic organizers facilitate learning in all students but more specifically for the Type 1 learner (4MAT). The organizers provide the visual aid they need.

There are several different types of graphic or visual organizers. The following are some of the more common ones.

Name of the Organizer	Examples
target	
right-angle	
Venn	
pie chart	
the web	
concept/mind map	

Reference: Novak, Joseph D., 1990. Concept maps and Venn diagrams: two metacognitive tools to facilitate meaningful leaning. *Instructional Science* 19: 1, 29-52.

Several examples of visual organizers, based on plants, follow.

Teacher Activity 8.2 (continued)

1. GENERAL INTRODUCTION (CONCEPT MAP)
   Question: Brainstorm photosynthesis: where does it occur, and what are its reactants and products?

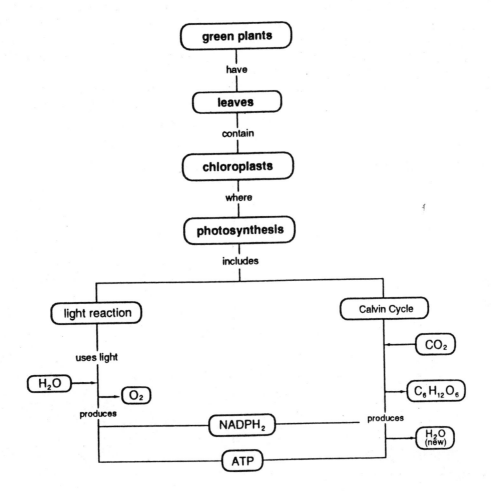

2. REVIEW OF A CONCEPT OR UNIT (VENN DIAGRAM)
   Question: Compare and contrast photosynthesis and respiration.

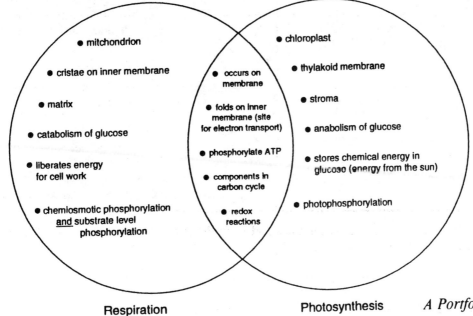

Teacher Activity 8.2 (continued)

3. COURSE REVIEW (CONCEPT MAP)
    Question: How are the following related: plants, animals, protists and fungi, climate, abiotic factors, and humans (as manipulators)?

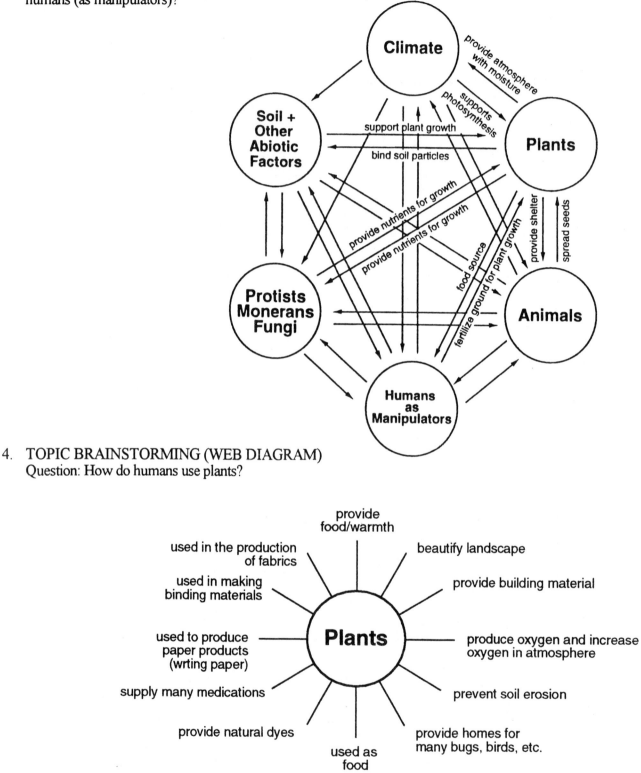

4. TOPIC BRAINSTORMING (WEB DIAGRAM)
    Question: How do humans use plants?

Student Activity 8.3 Energy Systems Assignment

Teacher Background

The Logistics

This assignment can be used in the Energy Systems section of any science course. It deals with typical research material in a new, creative, cooperative, fun way. Students generally need two class research/meeting periods and meeting time outside of class. The suggested time for completion is approximately 3 to 4 weeks.

This assignment is designed to incorporate several learning styles. The creative aspect is intended to draw out those students who are primarily 4R learners, while the research and write-up cater to 2L learners. (Please see Activity 1.3 for brief descriptions of each type of learner, and Bernice McCarthy's *The 4MAT System: Teaching to Learning Styles with Right/Left Mode Techniques* 1987, for details.)

The assignment makes the students accountable within the group, even though it is not a true Cooperative Group Learning simulation. Each member realizes that they must contribute to the group, and with the amount of work to accomplish, this can only be done by breaking down the assignment into "fair" chunks. Allow the students to decide among themselves who does what, but by making them document this, it is hoped that they will divide the work evenly. By giving a written description of the work actually accomplished by each student, it is hoped that this will be used by the students as a reflection of their "work attitude." Each student has the chance to grade the other members of the group and perform a self-evaluation. The teacher grades the final project and tabulates the group grades for a total of 45.

Teacher Evaluation of Group Mobile

1. All components present
       0   1   2   3   4   5
2. Use of color
       0   1   2   3   4   5
3. Neatness & creativity, quality
       0   1   2   3   4   5
4. Written breakdown of work accomplished by each partner
       0   1
5. Written component submitted for each resource, complete to within spec
       0   1   2   3   4   5   6   7   8   9
                                 Total   /25

Teaching Notes

Student Activity 8.3 Energy Systems Assignment

Student Group Contribution Rating Scale

Fill the names of your group members on the lines below. Circle the grade you would assign to each of the members of your group. Be thoughtful and honest.

	Self	NAMES: _____	_____
Attendance			
1. was on time for all meetings	0 1	0 1	0 1
2. was prepared with all materials for all meetings	0 1	0 1	0 1
Performance			
3. worked cooperatively within the group	0 1 2	0 1 2	0 1 2
4. accepted and performed fair share of the assignment	0 1 2	0 1 2	0 1 2
5. worked within group-set standards on their part of the assignment	0 1 2	0 1 2	0 1 2
6. helped with the organization of group materials	0 1 2	0 1 2	0 1 2
Attitude	0 1 2	0 1 2	0 1 2
7. used positive criticism and language when working with the group	0 1 2	0 1 2	0 1 2
8. maintained a positive attitude when suggestions were made and compromised	0 1 2	0 1 2	0 1 2
9. worked well to stay on task			
	0 1 2 3 4	0 1 2 3 4	0 1 2 3 4
Overall Contribution			
10. a mark that describes how well person has worked within your group			
Total /20			

My Comments: _____

_____

_____

_____

Student Activity 8.3 **Energy Systems Assignment**

Task

To design and make a hanging mobile incorporating the four non-renewable and the seven renewable energy resources.

Method

Working in assigned groups of three or four, spend some time researching and planning your design of a mobile, and then create it.

Content

1. You must have some representation of all four non-renewable and seven renewable resources. How you do this is up to your group.
2. The moveable parts of the mobile must be visible from at least two directions, and must move as a mobile is expected to.
3. The size is restricted to 60 cm X 60 cm.
4. Each resource must be accompanied by a one-page description (submitted with mobile) that includes the following information:
   - how resource was formed (is formed)
   - how resource is harnessed for practical use
   - pros/cons of the resource use
   - history of the use of the resource
5. A written outline of the specific work that each group member intends to contribute to the assignment must be submitted on

   _____.
6. Due at the same time as the mobile is a description of what each person actually contributed, and how you could have improved your contribution.
7. Also due when the mobile is handed in is an assessment sheet from each group member. This sheet assesses the other group member's contributions to the project.

Evaluation

Student Group Contribution	/20
Teacher Evaluation of Group Mobile	/25
Overall Individual Grade:	
Part I + Part II =	/45

Teacher Activity 8.4 A Subject Integration Idea

The following is an example of some of the content
which could be included in the integrated topic,
"Building a Composter."

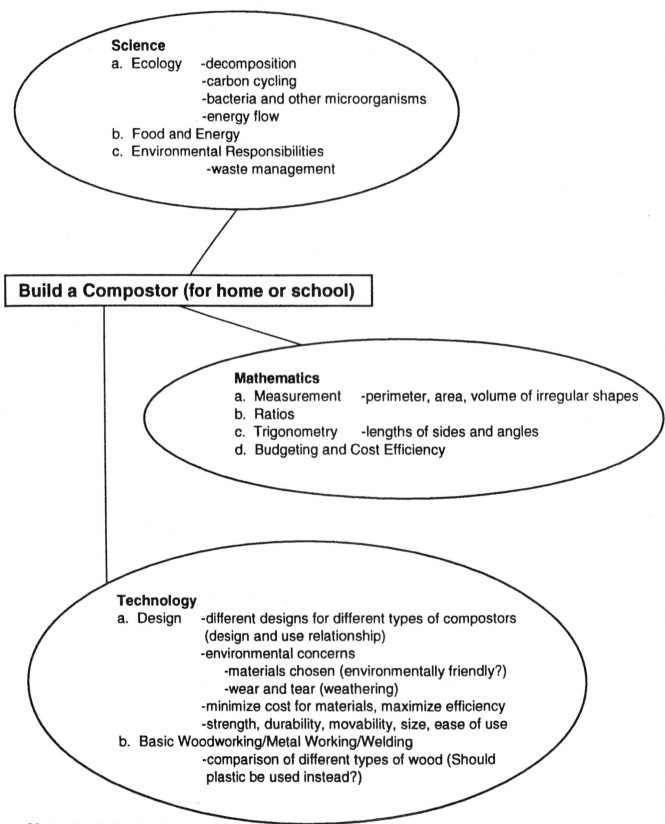

Science
a. Ecology   -decomposition
             -carbon cycling
             -bacteria and other microorganisms
             -energy flow
b. Food and Energy
c. Environmental Responsibilities
             -waste management

Build a Compostor (for home or school)

Mathematics
a. Measurement   -perimeter, area, volume of irregular shapes
b. Ratios
c. Trigonometry   -lengths of sides and angles
d. Budgeting and Cost Efficiency

Technology
a. Design   -different designs for different types of compostors
             (design and use relationship)
           -environmental concerns
               -materials chosen (environmentally friendly?)
               -wear and tear (weathering)
           -minimize cost for materials, maximize efficiency
           -strength, durability, movability, size, ease of use
b. Basic Woodworking/Metal Working/Welding
           -comparison of different types of wood (Should
            plastic be used instead?)

Teacher Activity 8.5 **Plague Generation: AIDS Awareness**

Overview

To carry out this activity, you must have access to the article, "The Plague Generation," by Richard C. Jones, which appeared in the November, 1993, issue of *The Science Teacher*. It describes an exercise that may prove valuable in encouraging AIDS awareness. The article provides background information concerning HIV, its transmission, and methods our society has used to try to arrest its spread. (See Appendix A.)

Discussion

In this article, ideas are provided for keeping the attention of students. Try to get dialogue going, but don't make it too fact-laden. Provide enough to answer questions, and use statistics sparingly.

Activity

An activity is described in the article. This has been used at several schools and met with success. Following the activity, students identify many interactive behaviors which became the focus of more discussion. A description of the activity is included here, followed by a short discussion.

1. This activity is a simulation. Students are to exchange "bodily fluids" three times, and then are tested for the presence of "infection."
2. Before class, prepare two cups, three for larger classes (24+), half-filled with dilute NaOH. Also prepare enough cups for the rest of the class, half-filled with water. (Use clear plastic cups.) Water looks and smells the same as dilute NaOH. The people with the cups of NaOH represent HIV carriers, and are unknown both to others and to themselves.

> **Safety Note:** NaOH is caustic so please ensure you use only a dilute solution and follow your school's safety procedures for its use.

3. Explain that the students are to exchange "fluids" with another student they "trust." This is accomplished by completely pouring the contents of their cup into another student's cup, and then pouring half of it back, thus ensuring complete mixing. This "exchange" is repeated with two more students.

4. After the exchanges, ask them if they trust the people they exchanged with. Have students hold up their cups, and add two or three drops of phenolphthalein to each. Make sure all of the students can see the results of each "test." In most cases, a majority of the class will have pink cups. This indicates they have come in contact with "the virus."
5. It would be timely to mention that surveys have indicated that students average three different sexual partners during their teenage years. This is why three exchanges were made.

Follow-up

6. Have students record the names of partners 1, 2, and 3. In this manner, the path of infection can be traced back to the original three.
7. Some students may form small groups and exchange only within this "community." Others may exchange with the same partner on each occasion. The advantages of these strategies for limiting "spread" should be discussed.
8. Monogamous relationships may be encouraged by demonstrating that only six people would be infected if all members of the class were monogamous in their exchange behavior.
9. You may want to discuss why the disease was initially contained within a sexually active homosexual community, rather than spreading evenly throughout North American society. However, it should be explained that it is not (nor ever was) a "homosexual" disease, but travels through channels of fluid exchange. Hemophiliacs, drug users, heterosexual partners, etc. — any such exchange of fluids can transmit the virus.
10. Graphs of the number of people infected may be drawn following the path of the three exchanges. The article provides a graph to illustrate this.

Extension

One or two students (popular would be best) could be instructed to "just say NO." At the end of the exercise, they could share how easy or difficult it was to just say "No." This is an example of peer pressure.

The social impact of this activity is further discussed in the article, as are sensitive issues the students might wish to discuss with you. Statistics are provided showing the number of cases in the U.S. and the world.

This is an excellent activity to use as a focus for a two- or three-day discussion on HIV transmission, strategies and methods to avoid contraction of HIV, and epidemiology of disease in general and HIV in particular. Discuss the problem of the long latent period of the virus, which means that many partners may be infected before the first carrier even realizes s/he is infected.

This is definitely a good activity for Quadrant 1, 3, and 4 learners. Follow-up in terms of calculations or textbook extensions may stimulate the Quadrant 2 learner.

Teaching Notes

Student Activity 8.6 Biology and the Internet

Your teacher will provide you with an Appendix of biology resources on the Internet. Check them out, and share your opinion of each with others in your class.

Your Mission

Select one site from those provided, and prepare a brief description to explain what it provides and its particular value. (Your teacher may assign sites to different students, depending on your interests.) If you selected your own site, find others in your class who chose the same site and combine your efforts to come up with the best possible description for the site. Then combine your site and description with those of other students in your class, and you will have a useful resource list for interest, study, and future projects.

New Sites I Like

(Add any new sites you find valuable here for your own use, and to share with others.)

_____

_____

_____

_____

_____

_____

_____

_____

_____

_____

_____

_____

_____

_____

_____

_____

_____

_____

_____

_____

_____

_____

_____

_____

Appendices

Appendix A

THE PLAGUE GENERATION
An Exercise in AIDS Awareness

Reprinted with permission from The Science Teacher, *November, 1993.*

by Richard C. Jones

High school students of the 1990s are unique in that they are coming of age during a worldwide plague. They have never known a world without AIDS and the Human Immunodeficiency Virus (HIV). Tragically, a survey of ninth graders reveals teenagers learn about AIDS mainly through their friends and television, while teachers, parents, and books are the least consulted sources.

As science teachers, we must be willing to discuss HIV and AIDS, even if the topics are uncomfortable and the obstacles are many. For non-specialists, the chemistry and microbiology involved in the HIV/AIDS cycle of infection can be intimidating. Indeed, after 12 years of intense research, producing more information on the AIDS virus than any other organism in the world, the exact triggering mechanisms for AIDS eludes scientists.

While it is helpful to understand the more general bio-chemical details when discussing the "plague," it is not a requirement for educating students about HIV and AIDS. What is vitally important is a thorough understanding of how HIV is and is not transmitted, and how students can protect themselves.

Surveys conducted by the Center for Disease Control (CDC),

show that 93 to 98 percent of teenagers are aware that AIDS is transmitted by sexual contact and IV-drug use. Unfortunately, knowledge of the "facts" does not appear to lead to behavior odification. Again, CDC surveys reveal most teenagers are sexually active during their teens (70 to 80 percent) but only 34 percent consistently use birth control. This figure may be even lower for HIV protection because the percentage of condom usage is not specified. This seems consistent with teachers' experience — knowledge in the abstract is not necessarily effective in altering teenage behavior.

The following activity initiates the connection between facts and behavior. It dramatically illustrates the geometries of a spreading pathogen such as HIV throughout a population, producing the Plague Generation. The impact of this activity increases with the number of students. Therefore I recommend combining classes when possible. Additionally, students will receive the most benefit from this activity if the methods for the transmission of communicable diseases have already been discussed in class.

THE MECHANICS OF TRANSMISSION
In this simulation, students exchange "bodily fluids" three times and are then tested for the presence of "infection". Smaller

classes may wish to begin the simulation with two "infected people" to generate more striking results. The following description is based on two infected people. The materials are inexpensive and easy to obtain (see Figure 1).

FIGURE 1. Materials for transmission demonstration.
- Clear plastic cups (8 ounce) — one per student
- Eye dropper or plastic pipette bulb — one per teacher
- Phenolphthalein — enough for a "squirt" (5-10 drops) per cup.
- Base Solution: NaOH, KOH, or other — ammonia is not recommended because of its identifiable odor. (200 mL of concentrated NaOH per 3 or 4 L of water produces appropriate base solution)

Safety considerations:
In high concentrations and for people with sensitive skin, a base solution such as this may irritate the skin upon contact. If contact is made, rinse with water. If there is no running water in the room, place a water bucket nearby where students could quickly dunk a hand.

Before class, fill two plastic cups half way with the base solution. These represent the infected carriers. Fill the remaining cups with an equal amount of water. The cups should be transparent so the "results" can be seen by the whole class. When class begins, distribute the cups randomly (or give each student a cup as they enter the room). Explain to students that two people (cups) in the class are HIV carriers, but that their identities are unknown.

Ask students to move around the room exchanging fluids with three other people in the group — people they trust. Students exchange fluid by completely pouring the contents of one cup into the other (thoroughly mixing the fluids), then pouring half of the volume back into the empty partner's cup. This is the first exchange. Students then repeat this procedure with two other partners so that three exchanges are completed.

Afterwards, have students take their seats and ask them if they trusted the people with whom they exchanged fluids. Instruct the students to hold their cups above their heads so everyone can see the results. Explain that the "AIDS indicator" (phenolphthalein solution) will cause the clear liquid in cups infected with "HIV" to change to a bright pink color. Dispense a few drops from an eyedropper into each cup. Swish the fluid around, and observe how many turn pink. Chances are that almost everyone will have a pink cup, in other words, will have come in contact with "the virus." This is an appropriate time to

interject that surveys reveal students average three different sexual partners during their teenage years — which is why students conduct three exchanges.

Select the first student to be tested carefully. All eyes are on them and they have a good chance of being positive. Students seem to remember this test but not necessarily the fifteenth test. Quickly drop the indicator into the rest of the cups so that no one is in the spotlight for too long. You can also have an assistant help dispense the indicator. Most students are amazed by the colorful chemical reaction, and also by the fact that they have been "infected."

After the excitement dies, you can repeat the exercise and ask students to record the names of their partners. Afterwards, students can trace the source of the infection by comparing list of partners. Additionally, ask the students to examine their list. If their list contains only same sex names, they represent the homosexual population in this demonstration. If their list contains exclusively opposite sex names, they reflect the heterosexual population. If their list has names

of both sexes, they symbolize the bisexual population.

This examination of who selected whom further illustrates how the pathogen crosses sexual preferential populations. This reinforces the fact that AIDS is not "just a gay disease," but has affected and is present throughout the entire population. Indeed, in September of 1993, the World Health Organization (WHO) estimated that between 40 and 110 million people will have become infected with HIV by the year 2000.

In subsequent exercises, direct students to calculate and graph the time for a pathogen to infect their entire class or school (Figure 2). As an extension, have them calculate and predict the rate of transmission for the first million diagnosed cases in the United States (Figure 3). Remember, these are only those reported to CDC and may represent only a small percent of the actual number. They will discover that both populations follow the classic "J" curve; a bridge into mathematics and graphing skills.

FIGURE 2. Time required to infect the student body.

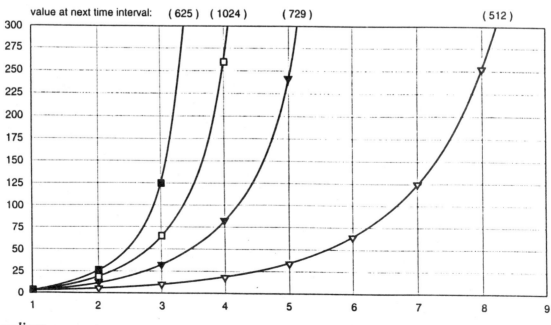

FIGURE 3. Growth of first million cases in the United States.

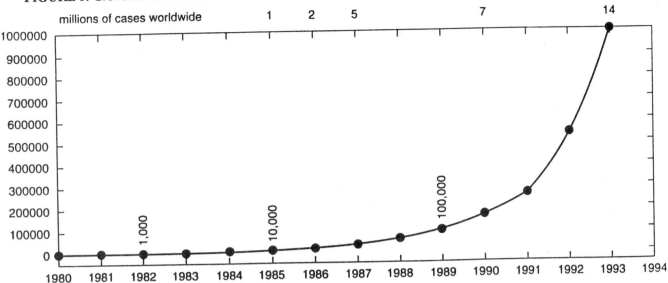

JUST SAY NO?

To illustrate the power of peer pressure, arrange for one student, usually of high status in the class (with an uninfected cup), NOT to exchange fluids with the other students. As the class is in the participatory spirit of the exercise, this individual has to resist the invitations of classmates. The student may or may not succeed in the "just say no" strategy.

At the end of the exercise, you can reveal your accomplice and have him or her relate to the class how easy or difficult it was to "just say no." Ask the other class members how they felt toward this person when he or she refused or attempted to refuse the exchange. Most students find this level of abstinence difficult. And if refusing to share a cup of water with another person is difficult, ask them to imagine the challenge when hormones, passion, and intense peer acceptance are involved.

REACTION

The reaction of "infected students" observing the few drops of phenolphthalein turning their cup pink follows a typical pattern: Denial, to anxiety, to scape-goating. Students may further reinforce this pattern by refusing to sit next to "infected" students in subsequent classes (even if the reluctant student has also tested positive). This became an excuse to make derogatory remarks and reassert the social pecking order. Interestingly, after this demonstration, several concerned parents called the school about the "AIDS Test." This was an index of how much students enjoy the drama of their parents' reactions upon learning their friends tested HIV positive. Additionally, it speaks to the effectiveness of the demonstration. Any science activity remembered past the bus ride home is a success.

SOCIAL IMPACT AND SCIENTIFIC LITERACY

Historically, people have responded to epidemics just as your students did: first denial, then anxiety and hysteria, followed by a search for a scapegoat. In biblical times, lepers were excluded from mainstream society. Leviticus 13:45-46 describes the manner lepers used to identify themselves in dress and speech to the uninfected. In 14th century Germany/Switzerland, Christians blamed the Jews for the bubonic plague and slaughtered whole communities. Syphilis and gonorrhea in 18th century Europe was known as the "French" disease by the English and Italians and the "Italian" disease by the French. The cholera epidemic of the 1830s was interpreted by religious fundamentalists as a judgment upon the poor and immoral.

The 20th century reveals similar patterns. In the early part of the century, polio in America was believed to be caused by Italian immigrants. In 1986, the townspeople of Ocilla, Georgia, learned HIV was in their community and implemented a policy of isolation for those individuals. A year later, in Arcadia, Florida, a couple's home was burned to the ground by angry "neighbors" who objected to the couple's HIV-infected children attending public school. In 1989, Andersonville, Indiana, fired one of its coaches who tested positive for HIV. In 1993, the U.S. Government quarantined HIV positive Haitian refugees in Cuba. Increasingly, students are confronted by similar irrational acts which heightens their anxiety levels. Teachers should try to counteract the effect of these sensationalistic media events by providing students with the facts about AIDS.

TALKING TO STUDENTS

Statistics about AIDS (Figure 4) are only frightening if you believe in them. This activity dramatizes and emphasizes the nature and rate of transmission. However, the primary defense is absorbing the message into behavioral patterns. This should be reinforced at every grade level; doubly so at the high school level where attitudes and behaviors are being cultivated. While there is no cure for AIDS, it is preventable.

Students need to hear about HIV and AIDS from responsible sources such as teachers and health professionals, but not in a lecture format or "preachy" tone. High school students often have begun to question the credibility of parents and teachers, and an authoritarian, "because-I-say-so" approach is generally not effective when trying to get students to listen. For example, rather than citing a list of their responsibilities as adults, discuss their right as people, such as their right to have accurate information to decide about their own behavior.

Most of their information concerning AIDS, which they feel is incomplete, comes from friends and the popular media (talk shows). Scare tactics have a minimal effect on this age group. They think of themselves as immortal because they have rarely had experience with long-term illness, terminal disease, and death.

Additionally, it is necessary to speak to them at their level of experience and reality. Most are already sexually active or experimenting. They are interested in protection, not abstinence. As difficult as this may be for the previous generation to accept, the "Just Say No" campaign has not been effective. Perhaps "Just Say Condom" is more realistic. Furthermore, communicate in a language they understand. While they need to know the vocabulary of science, "bodily fluids" and "sexual intercourse" may not translate into their domain. For example, they may not recognize that condoms are "rubbers."

KEEPING YOUR AUDIENCE

High school is a transitional period unlike any other. Trapped between being children and adults, adolescents bounce between each reality with great awkwardness. Some find it difficult to initiate or formulate questions. However, once the dialogue has begun, do not bombard them with facts. This can be overwhelming, confusing, and a "turn-off." Use facts and statistics like spices — just enough to make it interesting. Give them a moderate amount of information and time to allow the basic information to be absorbed. Questions will follow. Most of all, students need to understand that AIDS is a fatal condition. Presently, there is no medical cure, nor do researchers foresee any in the near future. However, once the virus is contracted, it will kill the host in a way that will devastate family members and friends — both emotionally and financially. Students must be reminded that the choices they make may actually be life and death decisions.

Discussing AIDS is difficult for most parents and teachers. It is clear that knowledge of facts alone does not change behavior. However, ignorance guarantees disastrous and tragic results. When 50 000 died in Vietnam, the nation felt compelled to build a monument. However, AIDS has already claimed that many victims in the United States, and another 200 000 will die within the next four years. If another monument is erected, it should be for the Plague Generation, reminding us of the price paid for ignorance and our inability to connect our behavior to our knowledge.

Richard C. Jones conducted this activity while teaching at West Orange-Stark High School in Orange, Texas. He can now be reached at Memorial Preparatory School, 2825 South First St., Garland, TX 75041.

FIGURE 4. AIDS statistics for students.

Number of AIDS cases diagnosed

Year	U.S.	World
1981	314	20 000?
1982	1 446	250 000
1983	3 901 (HIV isolated)	500 000
1984	7 863	1 000 000
1985	14 766	
1986	38 689	4 000 000
1987	48 825	7 000 000
1988	91 618	
1989	149 705	11 000 000
1990	227 670	
1991	351 715	14 000 000 (WHO estimate)
1992	1 022 784	18 000 000 (WHO estimate)
1995	3 050 000 (estimated)	
2000	5 200 000 (estimated)	20 to 25 million (CDC estimate)*

* WHO estimates are between 40 and 110 million

Fact: Once you have become infected with HIV, it takes an *average* of 8 years and 4 months for the first symptoms to appear. This is why you do not see many teenagers with full-blown AIDS. The symptoms of the disease will not become apparent until the teenage victims are in their 20s. In fact, in 1989, 17 220 cases were diagnosed among 20- to 29-year-olds. When did they contract AIDS? During their teens — mostly through sexual contact.

Fact: There is a belief that the AIDS epidemic is over or has peaked and is on the decline. The epidemic is reaching a crisis in the 1990s — especially among the young, poor, and women. Black women represent 11 percent of the U.S. population, but 51 percent of the AIDS cases involving women. Hispanic women represent six percent of the U.S. population, but 19 percent of the AIDS cases involving women.

Fact: Once infected with HIV, 20 percent develop symptoms within five years, 50 percent develop symptoms within ten years, 75 percent develop symptoms within 15 years, 95 percent develop symptoms within 20 years. What about the five percent that never show symptoms, yet are carriers of the virus? Carriers, with no symptoms, are the most dangerous people to the rest of the population. They are "invisible" to detection unless they elect to be tested.

Fact: Cases of AIDS in the U.S. are being reported at the rate of 50 000 to 80 000 per year. The number of cases doubles every 16 to 20 months. That is roughly one new case per class period for teenagers or roughly 180 new cases per day for the country.

Fact: You contract AIDS through sexual intercourse, or by sharing needles and syringes. HIV virus has also been found in saliva, but kissing has not been shown to be a risk factor for contracting the virus. There is, however, a theoretical risk of contracting the virus through oral contact if blood in the mouth of an infected person is contracted through the mucous membrane of his or her partner. There have never been any documented cases involving this type of transmittal.

Fact: There is no "safe sex" — just *safer sex*. Only latex condoms lower your risk and should be used with a sperm-killing foam, cream, or gel with nonoxynol-9 to further reduce risk of infection.

Fact: The more sexual partners you have, the greater your risk. You can contract HIV through just one sexual encounter. Don't be afraid to ask your partner's sexual history. Remember, a person can be a carrier for years and not show any symptoms. Twenty percent of high school students report having four or more sex partners.

Fact: One out of every ten girls under the age of 20 becomes pregnant in the U.S. each year; one out of eight is infected with a sexually transmitted disease every year.

REFERENCES

Center for Disease Control. 1989. *HIV/AIDS Surveillance*. Atlanta: U.S. Department of Health and Human Service.

Center for Disease Control. 1992. Sexual behavior among high school students — United States. *Morbidity and Mortality Weekly Report* 49(51,52):885-888.

Center for Disease Control. 1992. Sexual activity in high school students — United States. *Morbidity and Mortality Weekly Report* 49(52):122-124.

Cowley, G. 1993. The future of AIDS. *Newsweek*, vol.121, March 22, 1993, page 46.

Freitag, M. 1989. Citizen panel warns of failings in battle to halt spread of AIDS. *New York Times* 27:14.

Fineberg, H. 1988. Education to prevent AIDS: Prospects and obstacles. *Science* 239(4840):592-596.

Henshaw, S., and J. VanVort. 1989. Research note: Teenage abortion, birth, and pregnancy statistics; An update. *Family Planning Perspectives* 1(3):56-59.

Hirschorn, M.W. 1987. AIDS is not seen as a major threat by many heterosexuals on campuses. *The Chronicle of Higher Education* 4:1,6-8.

Hutman, S. 1990. AIDS: The year in review. *Aids Patient Care* 5(3):11-16.

Jessor, R. 1991. Risk behavior in adolescents: A psychosocial framework for understanding and action. *Journal of Adolescent Health* 7(12):597-605.

Luna, G.C. 1991. Street youth: Adaptation and survival in the AIDS decade. *Journal of Adolescent Health* 7(12):511-514.

Merson, M.H. 1993. Slowing the spread of HIV: Agenda for the 1990s. *Science* 260(May 28): 1266-1268.

Mosher, W. and O. Sevgi. 1991. Testing for sexually transmitted diseases among women of reproductive age: United States, 1988. *Family Planning Perspectives* 23(5):230-234.

Koop, C.E. 1988. *Surgeon General's Report on Acquired Immune Deficiency Syndrome (Update)*. Washington, D.C.: Government Printing Office.

Sorensen, A.A. 1990. Addressing the AIDS epidemic in the 1990s. *AIDS Patient Care*. 4(5):33-35.

Speece, S.P. 1992. AIDS education in the science classroom. *The American Biology Teacher* 54(1):13-15.

Verner, A.M., and L.R. Krupka. 1988. AIDS knowledge. *The American Biology Teacher* 50:426-431.

Weiss, R.A. 1993. How does HIV cause AIDS? *Science* 260(May 28):1273-1279.

RESOURCES FOR AIDS EDUCATION

PHONING FOR THE FACTS

U.S.A.

The Center for Disease Control:	(404) 330-3020
U.S. Public Health Service:	(800) 342-AIDS
National AIDS Clearinghouse:	(800) 458-5231
National Sexually Transmitted Diseases Hot Line:	(800) 227-8922
The Southern California AIDS Hot Line:	(800) 922-AIDS; Spanish: (800) 222-7432
Spanish AIDS Hot Line:	(800) 344-7432
National Safety Council:	(800) 621-7619, (Illinois) (312) 527-4800
Gay and Lesbian Youth hot line:	(800) 347-TEEN

Canada: AIDS Hotline Numbers

Alberta	800-772-2437
British Columbia	800-661-4337
Manitoba	800-782-2437
Newfoundland	800-563-1575
New Brunswick	800-561-4009
Northwest Territories	800-661-0795
Nova Scotia	800-566-2437
Ontario	800-668-2437 (French: 800-267-7432)
Prince Edward Island	800-314-2437
Saskatchewan	800-667-6876
Quebec	800-463-5656
Yukon	800-661-0507

ORGANIZATIONS

AIDS Action Council
2033 M St. N.W., Suite 802
Washington, D.C. 20036

American Association of Physicians for Human
Rights
2940 16th St., Suite 105
San Francisco, CA 94103

American Foundation for AIDS Research
5900 Wilshire Blvd.
Second Floor, East Satellite
Los Angeles, CA 90036-5032
or
1515 Broadway, Suite 3601
New York, NY 10036-8901

American Red Cross
Office of HIV/AIDS
Operations Department
1709 New York Ave. N.W., Suite 208
Washington, D.C. 20006

Center for Disease Control
1600 Clifton Road
Building 1, B-63
Atlanta, GA 30333

Canadian Aids Society
100 Sparks St., Ste. 400
Ottawa, ON, K1P 5B7
Canada

Canadian Public Health Association
National AIDS Clearinghouse
1565 Carling Ave., Suite 400
Ottawa, ON, K1Z 8R1
Canada

Consumer Information Center
Dept. ED
Pueblo, CO 81009
(Brochure: AIDS and The Education of our Children:
A Guide for Parents and Teachers)

Hispanic AIDS Forum
121 Avenue of the Americas, Suite 505
New York, NY 10013

National AIDS Clearinghouse
P.O. Box 6003
Rockville, MD 20849-6003

National PTA
700 N. Rush St.
Chicago, IL 60611
(Aids Brochure: How to Talk to your Teens and
Children about AIDS)

Surgeon General's Report on AIDS
P.O. Box 14252
Washington, D.C. 20044

WEBSITES

Canadian Public Health Association (National AIDS Clearinghouse): http://www.cpha.ca
Laboratory Centre for Disease Control, Health Canada: http://hpb1.hwc.ca/datahpb.data/lcdc/lcdcopen.htm
Center for Disease Control National AIDS Clearinghouse (Atlanta): http://cdcnac.aspensys.com:86
UNAIDS (United Nations agency responsible for AIDS): http://gpawww.who.ch/unaids/default.htm

BOOKS TO READ

Garvy, H. 1992. *The Immune System: Your Magic Doctor.* Los Gatos, Ca.: Shire Press.
Gallo, R.C. 1991. *Virus Hunting — AIDS, Cancer and the Human Retrovirus: A Story of Scientific Discovery.*
   New York. Basic Books.
Greenberg, L. 1992. *AIDS: How it Works in the Body.* New York: Watts.
Huber, J.T. 1992. *How to Find Information About AIDS,* 2d ed. NY: Haworth Press.
Hyde, M.H. and E.H. Forsyth. 1989. *AIDS: What Does it Mean to You?,* 3d ed. New York: Walker.
Kittredge, M. 1991. *Teens With AIDS Speak Out.* New York; Messner.
Quackenbush, M., and S. Villarreal. 1992. *Does AIDS Hurt? Educating Young Children About AIDS,* 2d ed.
   Santa Cruz, Ca.: ETR.
Silverstein A. and V. Silverstein. 1991. *AIDS: Deadly Threat.* Hillside, N.J.: Enslo.

Stimmel, B., S.R. Friedman, and D.S. Lipton. (Eds.) 1991. *Cocaine, AIDS, and Intravenous Drug Use*. New York: Haworth Press.

VIDEO

A is for AIDS, Revised Ed. The Altschul Group, 1992. Color, 15 minutes.

AIDS: The New Facts of Life/ ETR Associates, 1992. Color, 20 min. Teacher's guide.

AIDS — What Everyone Needs to Know. Churchill Films, 1990. Color, 19 minutes.

AIDS in your School, Revised Ed. The Altschul Group, 1992. Color, 21 min.

AIDS Babies. The Cinema Guild, 1990. Color, 58 minutes.

Between Friends. San Francisco Study Center, 1990. Color, 26 minutes.

Don't Get It! Teenagers and AIDS. Sunburst Communications, Inc. 1990. Color, 23 minutes.

Talking about AIDS. Perennial Education, 1990. Color, 30 minutes.

Teens Talk AIDS. PBS video, 1992. Color, 28 minutes. Includes: *AIDS: Trading Fears for Facts — A Guide for Young People.*

Appendix B
Model Cards for Student Activity 5.3

NAME:

SEX:

Genetic Traits

Blood type:

Color Blindness:

Eye Color:

Ear lobes:

Hitch-hiker's thumb:

Tongue rolling:

Right or left handed:

Hair Color:

NAME:

SEX:

Genetic Traits

Blood type:

Color Blindness:

Eye Color:

Ear lobes:

Hitch-hiker's thumb:

Tongue rolling:

Right or left handed:

Hair Color:

NAME:

SEX:

Genetic Traits

Blood type:

Color Blindness:

Eye Color:

Ear lobes:

Hitch-hiker's thumb:

Tongue rolling:

Right or left handed:

Hair Color:

NAME:

SEX:

Genetic Traits

Blood type:

Color Blindness:

Eye Color:

Ear lobes:

Hitch-hiker's thumb:

Tongue rolling:

Right or left handed:

Hair Color:

NAME:

SEX:

Genetic Traits

Blood type:

Color Blindness:

Eye Color:

Ear lobes:

Hitch-hiker's thumb:

Tongue rolling:

Right or left handed:

Hair Color:

NAME:

SEX:

Genetic Traits

Blood type:

Color Blindness:

Eye Color:

Ear lobes:

Hitch-hiker's thumb:

Tongue rolling:

Right or left handed:

Hair Color:

Organism and Clue Cards for Teacher Activity 7.2

Organism Cards

Fox

Wolf

Berries

Rabbit

Frog

Owl

Snake

Hawk

Mouse

Grain

Grasshopper

Grass

Clue Cards

1. Snakes are carnivores.

2. A wolf is a top carnivore.

3. Grasshoppers eat grain.

4. Rabbits do not eat grain.

5. Rabbits are herbivores.

6. Frogs eat insects.

7. Hawks eat both herbivores and arnivores.

8. Rodents eat grain.

9. Hawks do not eat rabbits.

10. Snakes eat rodents and amphibians.

11. Owls eat rabbits.

12. Snakes are eaten by birds.

Appendix C
Resources and References for Teaching Biology

The following is a collection of resources covering a variety of topics found in biology courses of study. Some of the resources are older publications but still useful, while others are very current. The list is by no means complete but rather a collection of places to turn to for a variety of techniques and hard-to-find pieces of information.

American Biology Teacher, National Association of Biology Teachers, 11250 Roger Bacon Drive, 19, Reston, Virginia, USA, 22090; the Journal of the American Association of Biology Teachers (USA) and a "must" for all biology departments.

Analyzing Issues in Science & Technology, Galbraith et al., in development, Trifolium Books Inc. Students learn strategies for analyzing issues and put them into practice. Facilitator Ideas booklet with additional case studies and news articles.

A Sourcebook for the Biological Sciences, Morholt, Brandwein, and Joseph, Harcourt, Brace, and Jovanovich Publishers, 1986. The classic reference for every biology teacher.

A Sourcebook of Biotechnology Activities, Rasmussen, A., and Matheson, R., National Association of Biology Teachers, 11250 Roger Bacon Drive, #19, Reston, Virginia, USA, 22090, 1990.

Basic Genetics: A Human Approach, 2nd ed.,BSCS, Kendall/Hunt Publishing Co., 1990. This is one of the very few genetics resources which deals with human genetics at the high school level. Includes a number of case studies.

Biodiversity, edited by Wilson, E.O., National Academy Press, 1988. Calls attention to the rapidly accelerating loss of plant and animal species to increasing human population pressure and the demands of economic development.

Biology Directions, Galbraith, D. et al, John Wiley and Sons Pub., 1992. This text, written for the Alberta Science guidelines is accompanied by a lab manual and teachers' guide with a number of novel lab activities.

Biology Discovery Activities Kit, Bellamy, Mary Louise, The Center for Applied Research in Teaching (a division of Simon and Schuster), West Nyack New York, 10995, 1991. A very practical, original activity book based on research into teaching.

Biology Labs That Work: The Best of How-To-Do-Its, NABT, A collection of the most popular lab tips and ideas from the American Biology Teacher journal.

Biology Research Activities, Newman, Barbara, Alpha Publishing Co., Inc., Annapolis, Maryland. Includes a number of interesting variations on traditional lab activities.

Biology on a Shoestring, Bellamy, Mary Louise, ed., National Association of Biology Teachers, 1995. A novel collection of 15 inexpensive labs focusing on ways of thinking, devising, and creating labs.

Biology Teacher's Survival Guide, Fleming, Michael, NSTA Publication Sales, 1840 Wilson Boulevard, Arlington, Virginia, 22201-3000, USA.

Biological Sciences Curriculum Study (BSCS), Pikes Peak Research Park, 5415 Mark Dabling Blvd., Colorado Springs, Co., USA, 80918-3842. An American organization dedicated to the improvement of biology teaching. Excellent source of varied teaching texts and resources.

Carolina Biology Readers, Carolina Biological Co. This is a series of articles, rather like the Scientific American offprints, covering a range of current topics. An excellent source of information for student projects.

Cranial Creations, Downing, Charles, and Miller, Owen, J. Weston Walch, Pub., 1990. A collections of 45 cooperative learning activities for biology classes.

Developing Biological Literacy: A Guide to Developing Secondary and Post-Secondary Biology Curricula, BSCS, Attn.: CAT, 830. Tejon St., Suite 405, Colorado Springs, CO 80903. A new resource from the staff of BSCS.

DNA Science: A First Course in Recombinant DNA Technology, Micklos, D., and Freyer, G. Carolina Biological Co., 1990.

Favorite Labs from Outstanding Teachers, Volumes I and II, NABT, 11250 Roger Bacon Drive, #19, Reston, Virginia, 22090-5202, USA. Contains original activities for high school level biology students, compiled from recipients of NABT's outstanding Biology Teacher Award.

Food Additives: Questions and Answers and Food Additive Dictionary are both available free from Health and Welfare Canada offices.

The 4MAT System: Teaching to Learning Styles with Right/Left Mode Techniques. McCarthy, Bernice, Excel Ltd. Barrington ll., 1987. Describes the 4MAT model and includes examples of lesson plans.

Genetics and Heredity, Newton, David, J. Weston Walch, Pub., 1989.

A Guided Tour of the Living Cell, de Duve, Christian, W.H. Freeman and Co.; a two-volume very unique treatment of cell structure-function, 1984.

Handbook of Research on Science Teaching and Learning, National Science Teachers' Association, Dorothy Gabel, (Ed.), 1994. If you are looking for one book dealing with research into teaching and learning in science, this is the one.

High School Biology, Today and Tomorrow, Rosen, Walter G., ed., National Research Council (US), National Academy Press, Washington, D.C., 1989. A fine collection of articles by educators and researchers in the field of education; covers a range of current topics and issues.

Idea Bank Collation, Talesnick, Irwin, S17 Science Supplies and Services, Box 1591, Kingston, Ontario, K7L 5C8. An excellent source of ideas for all sciences.

Investigations in Applied Biology and Biotechnology, Freeland, Peter, Hodder and Stoughton Publishers, 1990. An interesting compilation of labs and activities, including numerous quantitative labs.

Issues of Curriculum Reform in Science, Mathematics, and Higher Order Thinking Across the Disciplines, Office of Research, U.S. Department of Education, U.S. Govt. Printing Office, Order Desk: 202-783-3238.

Learning Biology With Plant Pathology, NABT, 1994. Anumber of activities which will make the learning of plant structure and function more relevant to students.

Low Budget Biology, Bert and Lynn Marie Wartski, 9612 Barton's Creek Road, Raleigh, North Carolina, 27615, USA. A unique collection of classroom ready ideas for teaching such biology topics as microbiology, DNA and genetics, evolution, etc. $50 US.

Multiculturalism in Mathematics, Science, and Technology: Readings and Activities, published by Addison Wesley and also available through NSTA.

National Association of Biology Teachers, 11250 Roger Bacon Drive, #19, Reston, Virginia, USA, 22090. This organization is a source of many valuable materials for the biology teacher.

National Science Education Standards, National Committee on Science Education Standards and Assessment, National Research Council, 1995, National Academy Press. Offers a coherent vision of what it means to be scientifically literate, describing what all students regardless of background or circumstance should understand and be able to do at different grade levels in various science categories.

One-Minute Readings, Brinkerhoff, Richard, NSTA Publication Sales, 1840 Wilson Boulevard, Arlington, Virginia, 22201-3000, USA. Opportunities to apply real world problems to the study of science.

Openers for Biology Classes, Gridley, Robert, Carolina Biological Supply Co., 1990.

Planning and Managing Dissection Laboratories, NSTA, developed by the Florida Assocaition of Science Teachers, 1994. A fine, compact book for novices adn veterans alike.

Plants in the Laboratory, Zuerner, F., and A. Camosy, NABT, 1984. A brief collection of new plant labs to illustrate a number of points. The National Association of Biology Teachers (US) produce a number of excellent resources, in addition to their magazine, The American Biology Teacher.

Plant Propagation, Philip McMillan Browse, Boreal Laboratories Ltd., 399 Vansickle Road, St. Catharines, Ont., L2S 3T4. With this book, you will be able to proagate any plant in your classroom or garden.

Population: A Lively Introduction, McFall, Joseph A., Population Reference Bureau, Washington, D.C., 1991.

Population Reference Bureau, 2213 M Street, N.W., Washington, D.C., 20037
The source for any information pertaining to the world population issue. Particularly useful is the annual world population data sheet.

Prudent Practices in the Laboratory, Committee on Prudent Practices for Handling, Storage, and Disposal of Chemicals in Laboratories, National Research Council, National Academy Press, 1995. Step by step planning procedures for safe handling, storage, and disposal of chemicals.

Roman's Notes on DNA, Romaniuk, Roman, in development, Trifolium Books Inc. A great little book of memory tricks and easy-to-read information on DNA. Also a comprehensive "state-of-the-art" glossary of over 280 DNA-related, frequently used terms.

Teaching Evolution as a Lab Science, NABT, 1994. A collection of paper and pencil labs on evolution.

The Responsible Use of Animals in the Classroom, Including Alternatives to Dissection, NABT, 1990.

Science Curriculum Resource Handbook, Kraus International Publications, available from NSTA Publications Sales, 1742 Connecticut Ave., NW, Washington, D.C. 20009, USA. An extremely useful resource for curriculum developers and teachers.

Science and Creationism: A View from the National Academy of Sciences (CLS), National Academy Press, 1992. This title continues to be a popular source for educators struggling with appropriate inclusion of information in their classrooms.

Science and Societal Issues: A Guide for Science Teachers, Barman, Charles et al, Iowa State University Press, Ames, Iowa, 1981. If you can find it, an excellent little book!

Science and Social Issues, Newton, David, J. Weston Walch Pub., 1992; available from MIND Resources Ltd., Box 126, Station C, Kitchener, Ont., N2G 3W9

Science and Society, Stahl, Nancy, and Stahl, Robert, Addison-Wesley, 1995. A fine collection of decision-making episodes for exploring society, science, and technology.

Science and Technology in Society, The Association for Science Education, College Lane, Hatfield, Herts AL109AA, U.K. This series, often referred to as the SATIS program, is a collection of case studies, background information, and exercises dealing with a variety of science and technology issues. Must presently be ordered directly from the U.K.

Science Books and Films, AAAS, P.O. Box 3000, Dept. SBF, Denville, NJ, USA, 07834. An excellent way to keep abreast of new teaching resources. Consider a school library subscription.

Science for All Americans, Rutherford, F. James, and Ahlgren, A., Oxford University Press, 1991.

Science for All Cultures, NSTA Publication Sales, 1840 Wilson Boulevard, Arlington, Virginia, 22201-3000, USA. Articles on multiculturalism and science from "The Science Teacher".

Science Teacher's Choice: Research Activities That Work, Williamson, Nancy, Broadview Press, Peterborough, 1989. A good source of ideas and activities related to library research and independent study work.

Scope, Sequence, and Coordination of Secondary School Science, Volume 2, NSTA, 1992. This volume examines relevant research related to how secondary students best learn science.

The State of the World, 1996, Brown, Lester R. (Ed.), W.W. Norton Co., 1996. An overview of environmental issues taken from a global perspective. This volume focuses on sustainable development.

Teaching Critical Thinking Skills in Biology, NABT, 11250 Roger Bacon Drive, #19, Reston, Virginia, 22090-5202, USA. This monograph provides practical techniques and procedures for teachers to apply in the classroom to help foster students' critical thinking skills.

Technology, Genetic Engineering, and Society, Keiffer, George H. National Association of Biology Teachers, USA; a monogram dealing with current biotechnology issues.

The Teacher's Complete & Easy Guide to the Internet, Heide, Ann and Linda Stilborne. Trifolium Books Inc., 238 Davenport Road, Suite 28, Toronto, Ontario, Canada, 1996. Great project ideas, teacher hints, and easy to follow text and graphics.

Together We Learn, Clarke, Judy et al., Prentice-Hall Publishers; a good first book on cooperative learning and how it might be used effectively in all subject areas.

Using Fast Plants and Bottle Biology in the Classroom, NABT, 1992. The instructional materials, developed by the National Council for Agricultural Education are excellent.

Wetlands, Committee on Wetlands, Characterization, National Research Council. Explores how to define wetlands and discusses the diverse and beneficial hydrological and ecological functions of wetlands, including irregularly flooded sites.

Working With DNA and Bacteria in Precollege Classrooms, NABT, 11250 Roger Bacon Drive, #19, Reston, Virginia, 22090-5202, USA. Contains 21 original activities ready for biology teachers to use in the classroom or laboratory - for students of all levels.

World Resources 1992-93: A Guide to the Global Environment, A Report by the World Resources Institute, Oxford University Press, 1992. A fine collection of U.N. Environmental and Development data, useful for a variety of units and courses.

For National Academy Press titles, in the United States order directly from the National Academy Press. In Canada, send, fax, or e-mail your order to

Trifolium Books Inc.
238 Davenport Road, Suite 28
Toronto, ON, M5R 1J6
Tel: 416-960-6487
Fax: 416-925-2360
e-mail: trising@io.org

National Academy Press
2101 Constitution Avenue, NW
Lockbox 285
Washington, DC 20055
Tel: 1-800-624-6242
Fax: 202-334-2451

Titles No Longer In Print

The following titles are no longer in print. However, if you are fortunate enough to run across a copy in a library or used bookstore, they are all excellent sources for classroom ideas.

Adventures With Small Animals, Bishop, O., John Murray Pub., Can. agent is Irwin Pub. A collection of activities suitable for the Int./Sr. Division; very well done.

Adventures With Small Plants, Bishop, O., details as above. Variations on many traditional labs.

Animal Care from Protozoa to Small Mammals, Orlans, B., Addison Wesley Pub., 1990. Everything that you need to know about animal care.

Biological Science Casebook, Newton, D., J. Weston Walch, Publisher. An older but fine collection of case studies dealing with many issues relating to biology and society. Deals with abortion, human life, pollution, population, etc.

The Eighth Day of Creation, Judson, H.F., Simon and Schuster, 1979. A fine resource book for a teacher in search of a historical account of the DNA story.

Simple Experiments in Biology, Bibby, Cyril, Heinemann Educational, London. A wonderful collection of ideas around which labs can be developed. The ideas, each usually a paragraph in length are arranged under traditional topic headings - in short, a biology "Idea Bank."

TVOntario Biology Programs

TVOntario has produced six biology series in a videotape format, as follows:

Homeostasis

This six-part, mini-series, explores the internal systems of balance in animals, using a computer graphics, cartoon-type format. Sequences illustrate how the body deals with stress and copes with changing conditions such as high and low temperatures, and how the shortage or excess of fluids is adjusted and regulated. Computer animation permits detailed analysis of biological processes such as the sodium/water cycle. Each of the six programs is approximately 10 min long and the series is accompanied by an excellent teacher's guide.

Energy Flow

This series encompasses one of the principal themes of any biology course: the flow of energy throughout the world of living things. Central to this concept is the process of photosynthesis, without which life, as we know it, could not exist. The series also deals with energy at the level of organisms, energy flow within a cell, and the important role of energy within our agricultural system. The six-part series concludes with a look at energy flow in the biosphere. An Energy Flow teacher's guide is also available.

Protein Synthesis

This is yet another six-part series, designed for a second-year Biology or Advanced Placement course. All six programs can be purchased on a single one-hour videotape, on the format of your choice. The six programs deal with protein structure, DNA - the molecule of heredity, DNA replication, RNA synthesis, the role of transfer RNA, and finally, ribosomal RNA. The series makes excellent use of computer graphics, bringing to life a topic area which is difficult to teach. The accompanying teacher's guide has a number of related lab exercises and up-to-date references.

Organic Evolution

Beginning with the Biblical account of creation, this animated mini-series relates the historical development of the theory of evolution. The series focuses on the work of Charles Darwin, Gregor Mendel and includes a section on the Hardy-Weinberg law. The series concludes with a modern synthesis of organic evolution.

Photosynthesis

This is a development of photosynthesis, including the chemistry of the process, suitable for the OAC Biology course. It is a six-part series, each program is approximately 10 min long.

Cellular Respiration

Another six-part series for a second-year Biology or Advanced Placement course.
See also, Organic Chemistry for a program called, "A Harvest of Enzymes".

All of the above are very reasonably priced. For further details, contact:

In Canada:
TVOntario Customer Service
Box 200, Station Q
Toronto, Ontario
M4T 2T1

In the U.S.A:
MTV
1515 Broadway 21st Floor
New York, NY
10036

Appendix D
Biology And The Internet

Netscape is the cadillac of web software which can enable you to contact a wealth of resources on the World Wide Web. Once in Netscape, you will see a number of "search engines" additional pieces of software, embedded in Netscape, which will let you search for any imaginable topic. Some of the search engines include "Web Crawler", and "Yahoo". Once underway, simply type in your topic, sit back and wait for the computers to talk to one another; this, in turn, will usually give rise to a number of resources and links to other sites and resources. Be forewarned, however: surfing the net can be very addictive. It's best not to do it on a school night or you might not make it to class the next morning!

The addresses of some good, specific sites for biology resources on the Internet are as follows:

Description	Address
Access Excellence (Genentech, Inc.)	http://www.gene.com/ae
American Institute of Biological Sciences	gopher://aibs.org
Bio Sci. Home Page	http://biosci.ohio-state.edu
Biotechnology and Biology	http://biotech.chem.indiana.edu/pages/contents.html
Birding on the Web	http://compstat.wharton.upenn.edu:8001/~siler/birding.html
The Birmingham Zoo	www.bhm.tis.net/zoo/
Carolina Biological Supply Company	http://www.carosci.com/carosci/
Cells Alive	http://www.comet.chv.va.us/quill/
Chicago Field Museum of Natural History	http://www.bvis.vic.edu/museum/
Dinosaurs--Field Museum of Natural History	http://www.bvis.uic.edu/museum/
The Dinosaurs of Jurassic Park	http://sln.fi.edu/tfi/info/current/dinosaur.html
Dinosaur skeleton site	http://tigger.jvnc.net/~levins/hadrosaurus.html
Discovery Channel Online	http://www.discovery.com
Dissecting a frog using computer-based 3D visualization	
	http://george.lbl.gov/ITG.hm.pg.docs/Whole.Frog/
The Dolphin Page	http://wjh-www.harvard.edu/~furmansk/dolphin.html
Eisenhower National Clearinghouse for Math and Science	http://www.enc.org
Electronic Prehistoric Shark Museum	http://turnpike.net/emporium/C/celestial/epsm.htm
Electronic Zoo	http://netvet.wustl.edu/e-zoo.htm
Fisher Scientific	http://www.fisher1.com
Frog Dissection	http://curry.edschool.Virginia.EDU/~insttech/frog (There are others!)
The Froggy Page	html://www.cs.yale.edu/
Genetics and Genetic screening	http://www.scicomm.org.uk/biosis/human/consent.html
Gordon's Entomological Home Page	http://www.ex.ac.uk/~gjlramel/welcome.html
Great Canadian Scientists Web Site	http://fas.sfu.ca/css/gcs/main.html
Hall of Health	http://www.dnai.com/~hohealth
History of the Light Microscope	http://duke.edu~tj/hist/hist_mic.html
National Science Teachers' Association (U.S.)	http://www.nsta.org
Introduction to Viruses	http://ucmpl.berkeley.edu/allifc/virus.html
Insect Hotlist	http://sln.fi.edu/tfi/hotlists/insects.html
Invention Dimension	http://web.mit.edu/invent/
Lesson plans for biology	
	gopher://ec.sdcs.k12.ca.us/11/lessons/UCSD_InternNet_Lessons/Biology
National Wildlife Federation Home Page	http://www.nwf.org/nwf/
Natural Resources Canada	http:/www.emr.ca
Nature Magazine	http://www.nature.com
New Bio Resources	http://www.library.wisc.edu/Biotech/resource/cumulative.html
New Scientist Planet Science	http://www.newscientist.com
North American Breeding Bird Survey	http://www.im.nbs.gov/bbs/
Ontario Science Centre	http://www.osc.on.ca

The Philadelphia Inquirer Health & Science Magazine	http://sln,fi.edu/inquirer/inquirer.html
Rainforest Site	http://mh.osd.wednet.edu/
Schoolnet	http://www.carleton.ca/english/schlnet.html
Smithsonian Institution	http://www.siedu/
The Virtual Fly Lab	http://vflylab.calstatela.edu
Virtual Fish	http://www.actwin.com/WWWVL-Fish.html
The Virtual Heart Tour	http://sln2.fi.edu/biosci/heart/html
Virtual TeleGarden	http://cwis.usc.edu/dept/garden/
Visible Human Project	http://www.nlm.nih.gov/extramural_reseach.dir/
Tour a dinosaur exhibit	http://www.hcc.hawaii.edu/dinos/dinos.1.html
Tree of Life Project	http://phylogeny.arizona.edu/tree/phylogeny.html
WhaleNet	http://whale.simmons.edu
Whale Watching Web	http://www.physics.helsinki.fi/whale/
Wolf Studies Project	http://informns.k12.mn.us/wolf.html

... for an excellent reference on how to use Netscape effectively, consider *Easy World Wide Web With Netscape* by Jim Minatel, published by QUE. Full color with super graphics and easy to follow text.

... and for a great reference with ideas on how to use the Internet effectively in the classroom, get a copy of *The Teacher's Complete & Easy Guide to the Internet* by Ann Heide and Linda Stilborne, published by Trifolium Books Inc. Great project ideas, excellent teachers hints, and easy to follow text and graphics, with over a thousand annotated online resources provided in an appendix.

Self Evaluation Form

Name: _____ Class: _____

Date: _____ Assignment: _____

	Always	Usually	Sometimes	Rarely	Never
Participation					
1. Participated well in group activity.	☐	☐	☐	☐	☐
2. Was present every activity period.	☐	☐	☐	☐	☐
Organization					
3. Prepared work ahead of time for the group.	☐	☐	☐	☐	☐
4. Did my share of researching material for the group.	☐	☐	☐	☐	☐
During the Group Sessions					
5. Assisted in the organization of the group time together.	☐	☐	☐	☐	☐
6. Stayed on task.	☐	☐	☐	☐	☐
7. Listened to the views of others.	☐	☐	☐	☐	☐
8. Sought clarification of ideas which I did not understand.	☐	☐	☐	☐	☐
9. Worked to resolve conflict when it arose.	☐	☐	☐	☐	☐
10. Helped to motivate the group.	☐	☐	☐	☐	☐
11. Made critical, yet non-personal comments.	☐	☐	☐	☐	☐
12. Carried my fair share of the work of the group.	☐	☐	☐	☐	☐
Completing the Task					
13. Met the deadline agreed upon by the group.	☐	☐	☐	☐	☐
14. Supported team members to complete their assigned tasks.	☐	☐	☐	☐	☐
Other (Be specific)					
15. _____	☐	☐	☐	☐	☐

Peer Evaluation Form

Group:_____ Class: _____

Date: _____   Assignment: _____

N.B.   Rate each group member on a 5-point scale where
       5 is the highest rating and 0 is the lowest.
       Use one column for each peer. Be sure to include
       the names!

	Name	Name	Name	Name	Name
Participation					
1. Participated well in group activity.	☐	☐	☐	☐	☐
2. Was present during every activity period.	☐	☐	☐	☐	☐
Organization					
3. Summarized his/her work from the expert group.	☐	☐	☐	☐	☐
4. Did his/her share of researching material for the group.	☐	☐	☐	☐	☐
During the Group Sessions					
5. Effectively presented the work from the expert group.	☐	☐	☐	☐	☐
6. Assisted in the organization of the group time together.	☐	☐	☐	☐	☐
7. Stayed on task.	☐	☐	☐	☐	☐
8. Listened to the views of others.	☐	☐	☐	☐	☐
9. Worked to resolve conflict when it arose.	☐	☐	☐	☐	☐
10. Helped to motivate the group.	☐	☐	☐	☐	☐
11. Made critical, yet non-personal comments.	☐	☐	☐	☐	☐
12. Carried his/her fair share of the work of the group.	☐	☐	☐	☐	☐
Completing the Task					
13. Met the deadline agreed upon by the group.	☐	☐	☐	☐	☐
14. Supported team members to complete their assigned tasks.	☐	☐	☐	☐	☐
Other (Be specific)					
15.	☐	☐	☐	☐	☐
TOTALS:......					

Activity Ideas and Notes

Activity Ideas and Notes

Activity Ideas and Notes

New Resources/Web Sites

New Resources/Web Sites

New Resources/Web Sites

TEACHERS HELPING TEACHERS SERIES

Dear Reader:

Has this book "worked" for you? We hope you have enjoyed using the ideas in *A Portfolio of Teaching Ideas for High School Biology*, and feel that by using these ideas in your biology classes, you have enhanced your students' problem-solving skills <u>and</u> desire to learn. We are pleased to have the opportunity to make this book available to you, and we hope you will find other resources in our **Teachers Helping Teachers** series, as well as Trifolium's other educational resources, of great value both to your students and for your own learning.

None of us are immune to the praise and criticism of others, and those of us who write, edit, and publish educational resources such as this one are no different. Please let us hear from you about, yes, *both* your criticism and your praise. We need to know what you find useful about each of our resources and what you would like to see developed differently. We are committed to producing exemplary resources that are truly useful to you. Thus, if you have any comments or recommendations that you feel would assist us in the development of future projects (and in future editions of this book), we welcome them. Please write, fax, or e-mail Trifolium at your convenience.

Do you have a project idea that you think other teachers would find helpful? If so, please send it to us for consideration. Our aim is to continue providing practical, effective educational resources, particularly in mathematics, science, and technology, and also in career development.

We look forward to hearing from you with your thoughts about this book, new project ideas, or both!

Yours sincerely,

Trudy L. Rising
President

Trifolium Books Inc.
238 Davenport Road, Suite 28
Toronto, Ontario M5R 1J6
fax 416-485-5563
email trising@io.org

And visit our Web Site:
www.pubcouncil.ca/trifolium

Teacher Notes

Teacher Notes

Teacher Notes

Teacher Notes

Teacher Notes

Teacher Notes